Torah Lights
Vayikra: Sacrifice, Sanctity and Silence

MAGGID

Shlomo Riskin

TORAH LIGHTS

VAYIKRA: SACRIFICE, SANCTITY AND SILENCE

Maggid Books

Torah Lights
Vayikra: Sacrifice, Sanctity and Silence

First Edition 2009

Maggid Books
An imprint of Koren Publishers Jerusalem Ltd.

POB 8531, New Milford, CT 06676-8531, USA
POB 2455, London W1A 5WY, England
& POB 4044, Jerusalem 91040, Israel
www.korenpub.com

ISBN 978 159264 274 8, *hardcover*

A CIP catalogue record for this title is
available from the British Library

Typeset by KPS

Printed and bound in the United States

To our beloved children

Batya and Eddie
Yosef, Mevasseret, Naomi and Akiva

Elana and Menachem
Avishai, Amiel and Elai HaKohanim

Hillel and Limor
Eden Barkai and Yaal David HaKohanim

Yoni and Limor
Shalev Hod Harel and Maayan Ivri HaKohanim
Nehora Yafit and Shoham Ahava

In the hope that they receive from us
a fraction of what I received
from my parents and grandparents

In profound gratitude
to my beloved friend

BERNARD GOLDBERG

for having sponsored this edition
of Biblical Commentary
to honor his mother

ELSIE GOLDBERG

Who has graced the world
for well over a century of years

Contents

Tribute   xiii

Introduction to Vayikra   1

VAYIKRA

When God Calls Twice: Two Separate Expressions of Summoning   5

The Small *Aleph* and the Great Soul   9

Uplifting The World   13

I Sacrifice, Therefore I Am   19

Sin and Responsibility   23

The Modern Significance of Animal Sacrifice   27

Does Judaism Believe in Democracy?   31

The Truest and the Hardest Sacrifice: Admission of Guilt   37

Prayers – Not Supplication, but Sacrifice   41

TZAV

Maimonides on Sacrifices, Revisited   49

Of Sinners and Saints   53

Deeds and Thoughts: In Ethics It's the Deed That Counts;
In Ritual, It's the Thought That Counts   57

What Does God Really Want of Us?   61

ix

SHEMINI

Brides and Grooms, Feasts and Fasts 67

When Extra Becomes Excessive: Nadav and Avihu As Sinners 71

The Difficult Lesson of Divine Distance: a Time
to Be Near, a Time to Be Far 77

The Message of Silence: Nadav and Avihu as Sacred Martyrs 81

When Does Wine Bring Sanctity, and When
Does Wine Bring Debauchery? 85

A Time to Speak, a Time to be Silent 89

You Are What You Eat 93

TAZRIA-METZORA

God, What Have You Done for Me Lately? 101

Love, Marriage and Continuity 105

Humans Must Perfect Themselves 109

The Miracle of Childbirth: A Brush with Death 113

Walls Which Speak in Red and Green 117

An Open Heart and a Closed Hand 121

AḤAREI MOT

Be Passionately Moderate! 127

How Yom Kippur Works 133

This World or the Next World – Which is Paramount? 137

Whose Life Is It Anyway? 143

KEDOSHIM

Marriage As a Loving Friendship in Sanctified Purity 149

What Does Holiness Mean? 153

How to Give Instruction 161

Who is the Neighbor We Must Love Like Ourselves? 165

EMOR

Kohen, Rabbi, Educator: A Proper, If Difficult, Job Description 175

Job Description Revisited 181

What We Are Willing to Die For Will Teach Us What to Live For 185

Martyrdom For the Sake of a Shoelace? 189

Justifying Martyrdom 191

The Truest Holiness Resides in Human Beings 195

Israel – The State, Jerusalem – The City of
Peace and Lovingkindness 199

The Passover Jew: The Beginning of a March
as a Family Member 203

The Shavuot Jew 209

When the Sabbath Silences the Shofar 215

BEHAR

Israel Is Married to Its Land 223

Count toward Purity 227

Jubilee: Salvation for the World 235

Jubilee Is True Freedom 239

The Land of Israel Is the Land of God 245

Does Our Bible Condone Slavery? 249

BEḤUKKOTAI

A Vision of Transformation 255

On What Merit Will We Be Redeemed? 261

xi

Biblical Commentators Cited in this Volume   267

Index of Biblical & Talmudic Sources   275

Tribute

I want to thank my revered teachers, Rabbi Joseph B. Halevi Soloveitchik, z"l, Prof. Nehama Leibowitz, z"l and Rabbi Moshe Besdin, z"l for their many insights into the words and commentaries of the Torah. Much of what is written here is based upon lectures and discussions I was privileged to have had with them – as well as with many great Torah scholars from whom I have learned throughout the years. Although I have attempted to give proper attribution so as to help bring redemption to the world, I am certain that there are insights I may have derived from others which I have come to think of as my own; suffice it to say that whatever may be worthy in this volume was derived from my teachers, but I assume complete responsibility for whatever may not be deemed worthy.

I am most appreciative to Sheldon Gewirtz, who originally urged me to begin writing a weekly commentary on the Torah portion, and to Jacob Lampert, who helped in the writing of the columns during the early years of this activity. The congregations I have been privileged to serve as rabbi and preacher, Lincoln Square Synagogue in Manhattan and the many synagogues of the City of Efrat, Israel, as well as my students at the Ohr Torah Stone Institutions served as the original sounding boards for these commentaries, which were then written and distributed in weekly columns for *The Jerusalem Post* and additionally in some thirty Anglo-Jewish newspapers worldwide. Hopefully, each additional rendering has helped improve my formulation and understanding.

My beloved family and extended family – and especially my cherished wife and life-partner, Vicky – have not only heard these ideas around the Sabbath table, but have also questioned them, argued with them and certainly refined them.

Most of all, I must give tribute to the Almighty, who has enabled me to labor in the vineyard of Torah during these last forty years as rabbi and educator, a calling which has made the Five Books of the Torah my constant guide and companion.

כִּי אִם בְּתוֹרַת ה׳ חֶפְצוֹ וּבְתוֹרָתוֹ יֶהְגֶּה יוֹמָם וָלָיְלָה

Introduction to Vayikra

his third book of the Bible, Vayikra (from the opening Hebrew word *"And [God] called* to Moses from the Tent of Meeting") or Leviticus (Latin for "pertaining to the Levites," the descendants of the tribe of Levi who served as priests and ministers of the holy Temple), is called the Book of the Holy (*Sefer haKedusha*) by the Talmudic sages.

The expressions of holiness which we find throughout this book is a far cry from Rudolf Otto's *Idea of the Holy* and its concentration upon the mystical and other-worldly awe-some and awe-ful "numinous"; the biblical concept of the sacred is much more down – to – earth, revealing a human "rendezvous with the divine" from within the context of Sabbath and festival familial celebrations (sanctity of time), from the experience of serving, communicating with and sacrificing to the divine in special centers of Sanctuary, Temple and synagogue (sanctity of space), but especially from our daily interactions with our fellow human beings – our spouses, our children, our neighbors and the strangers in our midst – from the actions and words which unify and ennoble personal relationships (sanctity of the human being). Holiness in the Bible is not so much leaving this world to reach out for the divine up there as it is our challenge to bring God into our every-day life down here, to re-make this world into a fitting place for His presence.

This third biblical book also deals with sacrifice – including the ultimate sacrifice unto death for an ideal, for a God, for a national future. And I must add that from a personal perspective the most difficult and even agonizing aspect of my rabbinate in Efrat is attempting to comfort parents whose children have lost their lives in defense of our homeland, in terrorist attacks. Nothing is as painful as a parent burying a child. Here too this book of the Bible provides direction and even comfort – especially in its confirmation of the human need to express emotion and even anger and in its acceptance of the necessity of silence in order to retain our often difficult relationship with the divine. Sanctity, sacrifice and silence are indeed the hall-mark of this most profound and relevant book of Vayikra, the call of the divine to His children on earth.

Vayikra

When God Calls Twice: Two Separate Expressions of Summoning

> *And God called to Moses and He spoke to him from the Tent of Meeting saying…*
>
> LEVITICUS 1:1

The portion of *Vayikra* opens with two separate expressions of "summoning" – "And God *called* to Moses and he *spoke* to him." Why are there two distinct expressions, to call and to speak? Perhaps one may suggest that this parallels the divine repetition of Moses' name at the burning bush, when the Almighty cries out "Moses, Moses" which the Midrash usually explains as being a repetition of affection. When I look back however upon my own early years, whenever one of my parents called my name twice (at that time it was "Steven, Steven"), it generally meant that I was in trouble for something I had done that was not particularly appreciated by the older generation. Why do we therefore assume that in this case of Moses the repetition reflects affection rather than anger?

The truth is that the Midrash in the beginning of this Torah portion presents another explanation. At the end of the book of Exodus, the Torah describes a cloud which descended upon the Tent of Meeting, a cloud which symbolized the Divine Presence. The Torah likewise insists that no one – not even Moses – could enter this divine cloud without being especially invited by God to do so. Hence, suggests the Midrash, God had to call out to Moses to permit him to enter the cloud, after which God spoke and communicated a specific message.

This explanation not only interprets the repetition of the divine summons but also provides a most profound and magnificent symbolism expressing the divine challenge to humanity. The Almighty appears as a cloud; we apprehend Him only "through a glass darkly." Perhaps the reason why our God has neither shape nor form and is not clearly defined in any physical way is in order to teach that those who follow such a God must be prepared to chart new territories and to enter undefined areas. Our God created a world which contains chaos so that we can make order of it and He formed that world with evil so that we may perfect it in the Kingship of God. We must enter the nebulous and the unknown and bring God's presence into areas in which He is not yet manifest. Egypt was a clearly defined society with a specific caste system of masters and slaves, lordly Pharaohs and abject subjects. We followed an unknowable God into an unknown desert in order to bring out His divine word (*dibbur*) into the arid wasteland (*midbar*).

> A voice called out in the desert: prepare a place for the Lord, make a straight pathway in the desert for our God.
>
> Isaiah 40:3

And so does the prophet Jeremiah praise Israel:

> I remember the lovingkindness when you were young, the love of your youth; you walked after me in the desert, in a land which was not yet seeded.
>
> Jeremiah 2:2

This is the ultimate challenge of the true person of faith: To enter unknown terrain and to bring the divine message of ethical and moral monotheism to a world that does not yet know it. This is the ultimate challenge of our life in Israel, filled as it is with uncertainty and danger. Israel the people, from the backdrop of Israel the land, must sanctify Jerusalem and proclaim from the holy Temple the message of world peace and human justice.

What gives the individual the strength and the courage to walk with God into the unknown and even to make a place for the Almighty in a wilderness? Perhaps if an individual really feels that he is being summoned by God, that he has a divine vocation – that he is being called by God to the extent that he feels a "calling" – then he goes forward into the cloud unafraid.

Given this understanding, I believe we have an even deeper insight into why Moses is summoned twice and why God repeats his name "Moses, Moses." The Midrash teaches us that every individual has a double image: He/She is the person that he/she is but is also the person whose image is imprinted in the divine Chariot (*merkava*) in the highest heavenly sphere. This double human identity is even given expression in two very similar blessings which we recite at weddings under the nuptial canopy. One blessing reads:

Blessed are you, the Lord our God, who creates the human being.

The second blessing reads

image - spirit of physical

Blessed are you, O Lord, who has created the human being in His image, and in the image of the shape of His form has He fashioned him as an eternal building. Blessed are you, O God, who creates the human being.

These two blessings are two aspects of every individual. First, each of us is born at a specific time in a specific place to a specific set of parents with a specific physical build and appearance, slated to live for a specific number of years. Second, each of us as a member of a historic nation, has a collective memory which extends backwards to Sinai and the Garden of Eden, as well as collective anticipation which extends forward to the messianic age. It is this second aspect of our personality which links us to eternity and enables us to transcend our specific time and place.

God summons Moses twice and calls out at the burning bush "Moses, Moses" because there are in reality two Moseses: the first person, Moses of Egypt, was a prince in Pharaoh's court and fell in love with the Midianite Tzipporah; the second person, Moses, spoke to God and sacrificed all of his princely comforts to link his destiny with his people and their redemption. In so far as the first aspect of our transient personality is joined to the second aspect of our transcendent personality we will have the capacity to meet God in the haziness of the nebulous cloud of the unknown. God calls Moses twice because it is the second Moses who has the courage to face uncertainty and, because of that, he has gained eternity.

The Small Aleph and the Great Soul

*And the Lord called to Moses and He spoke to
him from the Tent of Meeting saying…*

LEVITICUS 1:1

What may cause the countenance of a particular individual to
glow with a special charismatic radiance which sets him apart from all
others? Let us explore the origin of Moses' "rays of splendor" (Ex. 34:29),
sometimes inaccurately rendered as "horns" because the Hebrew word
keren can mean either ray or horn. As a result of this mistaken translation, Michelangelo's Moses is depicted with two horns protruding from
his forehead and the typical anti-Semitic canard is to portray every Jew
with horns. I believe that a deep understanding of this phrase – in correct
Hebrew translation – will shed interesting light on radiant appearances
in general and on Moses' unique personality, in particular.

The book of Leviticus opens with the verse, "And the Lord called
to Moses," the first word being the Hebrew *"Vayikra,"* which means "and
He summoned" or "called out to." It is fascinating that a small "aleph" is
the masoretic, traditional way of writing the Hebrew *VYKRA*, so that

the text actually states "*Vayiker*, and He chanced upon," as if by accident. Rashi comments: "The word *VaYiKRA* precedes all (divine) commandments and statements, which is a term of endearment used by God when He speaks to the heavenly angels; however, God appeared to the prophets of the idolatrous nations of the world with a temporary and impure expression, as it is written, 'And He chanced upon (*VaYiker*) Balaam.'" The picture portrayed by Rashi's midrashic commentary suggests that as Moses was writing the Torah dictated by God, he was too humble to accept for himself the more exalted and even angelic-suggesting divine charge of *VaYiKRA*; therefore, he wrote the less complimentary *VaYiker* relating to himself, while retaining his faithfulness to God's actual word *VaYiKRA* ("and He summoned") by appending a small aleph to the word *VaYiKRabbi*

The Midrash goes one step further. It poignantly, if albeit naively, continues this picture by suggesting that Moses, having completed his writing of the Five Books, was then left with a small portion of unused divine ink; after all, the Almighty had dictated *VaYiKRA* and Moses had only written *VYiKRa*, rendering the ink which should have been used for the regular size aleph as surplus. The Midrash concludes that the Almighty Himself, as it were, took that extra ink and lovingly placed it on Moses' forehead; that is what gave rise to Moses' "rays of splendor."

Behind this seemingly simplistic but beautiful description lies a world of profound thought. The Midrash is teaching that because Moses did not transfer all of the divine ink to the Torah parchment – obviously not, if we understand the ink to symbolize the divine will – there must have been many layers of ideas deeply embedded within the actual letters of Torah which Moses understood, but which was too profound for him to successfully communicate to others. As Maimonides explains in Section III of his *Guide for the Perplexed*, Moses was on the highest level of the ladder of prophecy; only he – and none other of his contemporaries – was able to fully comprehend the divine will. Moses wrote down and explained as much as he felt could at least be understood by Joshua and the elders; the rest, he retained within his mind and within his soul. The aspects of Torah which Moses retained within himself but did not write or speak are graphically expressed by the midrash as the extra ink placed upon his forehead.

Most people are less than they appear to be – or, at least, are less than what they would like us to think they are. They immediately try to impress us with what and whom they know, dropping names and terms which imply that they are far more learned and knowledgeable than they actually are. As another midrash describes it, they are like the pig who extends his cloven hoof as if to advertise, "You see how kosher I am, you see how kosher I am." If we look more deeply at the pig, however, we will readily discern that it is not kosher all, because it lacks the second necessary condition for kashrut: a double digestive tract. Based upon this midrashic image, Yiddish folklore refers to any individual who tries to impress others at a first meeting with how much he knows (when in actuality he knows very little), as "chazir fissel kosher," (the pig's cloven hoof gives an external appearance of being kosher).

Most people are less than they appear to be – and wear artificial masks as cover-ups in order to make a false impression; indeed *persona*, the base word for personality, is the Greek word for mask. There are, however, those rare individuals who are more than they appear to be, who have much more knowledge, insight and sensitivity than they would ever wish to – or feel that they are able to – communicate to others. It is that inner wisdom, hidden from the outside world of externals, which causes a charismatic glow of radiance to emanate from the countenance of such people. In the case of Moses, the concealed depths of his spiritual and intellectual understanding were of such a highly charged nature that they emanated rays of splendor which necessitated him to wear a mask – not to exaggerate who he was, but rather to minimize the divine sparks which his inner self naturally and automatically projected (Ex. 34:33).

Once we understand that the Torah which Moses received from God contained much more, eternally more, than he ever communicated in either written or oral formulations, we may begin to understand the powerful source for an unending and constantly regenerating Oral Tradition. Indeed, "Whatever creative interpretation a learned and devoted scholar-student may expound was originally given to Moses at Sinai" (*Vayikra Raba* 22:1). And at the same time, we now understand the real source of charismatic rays of splendor.

Uplifting The World

> *Speak unto the children of Israel and say unto them: When any person of you brings an offering unto God, you shall bring from the cattle, the herd or the flock.*
>
> LEVITICUS 1:2

The book of Leviticus continues where the book of Exodus left off: after the exquisite description of the complexity of the Sanctuary's components, the Torah is ready to introduce the priestly duties of sacrifices described in the verse above.

Undoubtedly, the entire sacrificial system, replete with whole burnt offerings, sin offerings, guilt offerings and peace offerings, has a rather raucous ring to the modern sophisticated ear.

Rabbi Samson Raphael Hirsch attempts to provide a symbolic significance for each of the sacrifices, and etymologically suggests that the essence of *korban* (Hebrew for sacrifice) is to bring the individual close (*karov*) to God.

For our purposes, I'd like to approach the entire holy Temple ceremony by analyzing a rather striking midrash which emphasizes an otherwise innocuous pronoun in our opening verse: "When any person of you (*mikem*) brings an offering unto God…." The fact is that if the purpose of our verse is to issue a command to bring offerings, it could just as easily have been transmitted without the word *mikem*. Indeed, this particular pronoun in this particular context never appears in the Bible again. Teaches the midrash:

> Why does [the biblical text] state *mikem* [of you]? From here we derive that whoever fulfils the obligation to recite one hundred blessings each day is considered as if he/she offered a sacrifice. How do we know this? From the Hebrew word *mikem* [of you], which has the numerical equivalent of one hundred [*mem-kaf-mem*=40+20+40].
>
> *Midrash Yalkut Ma'ayan Ganim*, ad loc.

Why does the midrash link these 100 daily blessings with an offering to God? Presumably, if we understand the connection, the world of blessings may very well illuminate the world of sacrifice.

Let us examine the essence of a blessing. Rabbi Yehuda HaLevi in his classic work *The Kuzari*, teaches that the laws of proper blessings enhance our pleasure, create heightened awareness and a more sensitized appreciation of every object in the world; indeed the necessity of our making a blessing precludes the possibility of our taking for granted God's many bounties. *The Kuzari* illustrates his concept by the analogy of a drunkard fortunate enough to have a patron. This drunkard, like all people, asked for and received special foods, vintage wines and splendid clothing. But as luck would have it, the patron's benevolence reached the drunkard during one of his binges. When he finally woke from his stupor, it was clear that he had no sense of having received anything from his benefactor. His mind – totally absorbed inside a bottle of illusions – had no memory and therefore no concept of what he had been given. Pleasure demands awareness, and a blessing sharpens our senses, leading them to appreciate what we have and are about to enjoy: a glorious sunrise, a burst of lightning, the children around the Sabbath or festival table, a bright, red strawberry.

But what then should we do with our awareness? How do we channel our new-found awakenings to the gifts of the world around us? A comment of Rabbi Aaron Soloveitchik, of blessed memory, on a passage in Tractate *Berakhot*, can provide us with an interesting insight.

> Rabbi Levi asked concerning two contrasting texts. It is written: 'The heavens are the heavens of God but the earth has He given to the children of men,' (Ps. 115:16), and it is also written, "The earth is the Lord's, and the fullness thereof" (Ps. 115:16). There is no contradiction: in the one case it is before a blessing has been said, in the other case after.
>
> *Berakhot* 35a

The usual interpretation explains that before I make a blessing, everything belongs to God; the blessing is my request for permission to partake of God's world. Hence, partaking of something without a blessing is in effect committing thievery against God; it is as a result of our blessing that the Almighty grants us permission to partake of His physical world. In effect, before the blessing, the world is God's, and after the blessing, He gives the world's bounty to us humans.

In a unique twist, Rabbi Soloveitchik turns this interpretation on its head: "The heavens are the heavens of God, but the earth has He given to the children of men." (Ps. 115:16) is the description of the world before blessings, and the verse, "The earth is the Lord's and the fullness thereof," is after the blessing!

Why? A world devoid of blessing is a world without any divine connection, a neo-platonic world with an iron curtain separating the human and godly realms. The spiritual belongs to the heavenly domain, to God, while the physical is the sphere of humanity – and never do the twain meet. But once the human being utters a blessing before enjoying any worldly gift or upon experiencing a special historical or natural phenomenon, humanity is admitting God into the world, it is suffusing the physical sphere with divine spirituality, and it is recognizing God's gifts within the material world.

Suddenly, earth and heaven are no longer enemies, strangers in a strange universe, but all of God's creations magnificently and miraculously come together. If the Torah has one urgent message, it is the sancitification of our physical world. For Jews, the divine and the physical meet in an eternal dialogue, and the first expression of that dialogue is the blessings we make.

An additional and related aspect of the significance of blessings is the Hassidic-Kabbalistic nation. Early in the book of Genesis, God becomes disappointed with His world and decides to destroy it (except for the righteous Noah, that is):

> And God said, "I will blot out the human being whom I have created…. both humans, and beast, and creeping things, and fowl of the air…."
>
> Genesis 6:7

Rashi asks why God's anger is directed toward animals? After all, these brute creatures are innocent of any wrongdoing. Rashi then presents us with two possible interpretations. First, that all of creation including animal life had become so depraved that nothing could be called inno-cent – a perversity that pervaded all of reality. But his second answer is the one that concerns us here:

> Everything was created for the human being. When he ceases to be, what need have I for them (beasts, creeping things, fowl)!
>
> Rashi, ad loc.

This is a profound idea that looks at God's creation as a hierarchy, start-ing with inanimate rocks, ascending toward living plant life, and from there to animal creatures of mobility and then reaching upward to the communicating human being. All the mobility of an animal cannot alter the fact that animals are ruled by the earth and the waters and the skies, into the mold of each individual species. Only the human being's gift of communication enables him to relate to God – if indeed he utilizes his freedom of choice properly.

Now when the human being takes the objects of the world around him, and he makes blessings over the world he lives in, he brings all of existence – including plant life, animal life, and every worldly object –

into a relationship with God. In effect he is giving a higher purpose to all of these realms, thereby bringing everything back to its ultimate divine source. By uplifting the world, by restoring it to its divine dimension, the human being repairs a world broken by iniquity and despair, alienation and materialism And without this potential for uplifting the world, without a lofty and up-reaching human being, all of creation becomes short-circuited, the universe has no purpose for being, a reverse "bang" takes place.

Now we are ready to return to our midrash, the rabbinic concept which identified the daily blessings with the sacrifices that brought humanity close to the divine. What God wants from us is not only to build a Sanctuary, but to transform the entire world into God's Sanctuary, God's Temple. "You shall make for Me a Sanctuary so that I may dwell in your midst," commands God. And so the sacrifices bring cattle, grain and fruits back to the Almighty who created them, enlisting the world – inanimate, vegetative and the human facilitators – in the service of the divine.

Just as Temple sacrifices brought God into the world in the period of the Sanctuary, so do the daily 100 blessings bring God into the world – suffuse the material world with divine spirituality – in our world today. By means of daily blessings we have the potential of making the entire universe a divine sanctuary.

I Sacrifice, Therefore I Am

> *Speak to the children of Israel, when any human being of you shall bring from themselves a sacrifice to God from the cattle, from the herd or from the flock…*
>
> LEVITICUS 1:2

What does it mean to be human? What defines our essence? Are we the "social animal" of Aristotle, or the thinking being of Descartes (*"cogito ergo sum"* – I think therefore I am)?

Clearly one can come up with a variety of definitions for the human, from the creature who loves for no reason to the creature who hates for no reason: I [insert almost any verb] therefore I am. Alternate the verb, and you create a myriad of possibilities.

I would like to suggest that the opening verses of the book of Leviticus present us with a different and somewhat surprising idea of what it means to be human, a *verb* that not too many people use, and certainly not the usual first-choice definition for the human spirit.

In effect, the verb I have in mind is the theme of the biblical book of Leviticus: "I *sacrifice*, therefore I am." I call this surprising because presumably we are searching for a universal definition of the human, and the sacrificial cult detailed in Leviticus is generally regarded as being rather parochial in scope, even primitive. So great is this perception or misconception that large segments of modern Jewry, intent on erasing all barriers between Jews and the rest of humanity and endeavoring to put only Judaism's best foot forward, have practically edited out all references to sacrifices from time-honored prayers in the prayer book and from Torah readings on festivals. But in their haste to whitewash Jewish texts, they sometimes overlook concepts whose underlying message strikes at the heart of human existential need.

Leviticus begins with God calling to Moses and presenting a command which is the theme of the entire book and perhaps of all life: "Speak to the children of Israel, when *any human being* (in Hebrew, *adam*) of you shall bring from themselves a sacrifice to God from the cattle, from the herd or from the flock ..." (Lev. 1:2).

Adam is, after all, the most universal term for person, since it evokes the first human who ever lived and from whom every single person in existence is descended, and is the root word of *adamah*, earth, from which all life emanates. Not only does *adam* seem out of place in this particular context, but if we remove the word *adam*, the verse still makes perfect sense.

Hence, the Torah is teaching that the essence of the human being is his need, and his ability, to sacrifice. Inherent in the logic behind this concept is the most fundamental aspect of the human predicament. Only the human being, among all other physical creatures of the world, is aware of his own limitations, reflecting on his own mortality. And since Adam is aware of the painful reality that no matter how strong, powerful or brilliant he may be, he will ultimately be vanquished by death, his only hope is to link himself to a being and a cause greater than he, which was there before he was born and which will be there after he dies.

Most people amass wealth and material goods in order to utilize them for themselves, to enjoy them in a physical, here-and-now sense. But mortality teaches that our material possessions do not really belong to us; one day we will be forced to leave them and the entire world behind, and they will often fall into the very opposite hands to those we would have liked to have received them. Hence the real paradox: only those objects which we commit to a higher cause, which we give to God, to His Temple, to His Study Hall, to His home for the sick, to His haven for the poor – only those are truly ours, because they enable us to live beyond our limited lifetime, perhaps to all eternity. Only that which we sacrifice is really ours!

The expressions of sacrifice are various, but common to building a yeshiva or funding a new hospital wing to ease the sufferings of humanity, is that both link us to a greater good, a hope for the future. I may die, but to the extent that I devoted my life to causes that will not die, that live on, then I also live on. Sacrifice makes it possible to bathe in the light of eternity.

Jewish history, and the City of Jerusalem, emanate from this fundamental truth present in God's initial command to Abraham to sacrifice his beloved son Isaac on Mount Moriah, known as the Temple Mount in present-day Jerusalem. Isaac was the first *olah* – whole burnt offering. In effect, God was teaching Abraham that his new-found faith would only endure in history eternally if he, Abraham, were willing to commit to it his most beloved object, ironically his very future. In his willingness to make that sacrifice, Abraham secured his religion's, and his own, eternity. And by means of the seminal story of the *akeda*, the Bible teaches that the most significant sacrifices of all are not our material goods, but rather are our own selves, our time and our effort, our intellects and our unique abilities. People must sacrifice "*mikem*," from themselves (Lev. 1:2). Giving a child the gift of a check is hardly as significant as giving a child the gift of our time, our personalities, our thoughts and our struggles. And this, too, God teaches Abraham. God ultimately instructs him not to slay Isaac, but to allow him to live, because the greatest sacrifice we can make is not in dying for God but is rather in living in accordance with His commands and desires. Isaac in life *after* he descends from the altar is called by our sages an *olah temima*, a whole burnt offering.

Strangely enough, the dean of biblical commentaries, Rashi, suggests another reason for the seemingly superfluous "adam" in our text. The Bible is teaching that just as Adam, the first human being, never sacrificed stolen goods, since everything in the world belonged to him, so are we prohibited from sacrificing anything which is stolen. Such a lesson certainly protects Jewish society against a Robin Hood mentality, which steals from the rich in order to give to the poor. The end doesn't justify the means, and we must always pursue justice by means of justice (*"zedek zedek tirdof"*).

But perhaps Rashi is protecting us against an even deeper, and more appealing, danger inherent in the idealization of sacrifice. We can only sacrifice objects or characteristics which technically, if even in a limited sense, belong to us. We dare not sacrifice innocent human beings, even if we believe that such a sacrifice will prevent the future murder of Jews. We cannot even immolate ourselves on a funeral pyre, commit suicide with the dying gasp, "let my soul die together with the Philistines." Our lives belong to God, and we dare not steal that which is His in our gift to Him. The end can never justify the means! We can only sacrifice ourselves in a manner, and for a cause, which He commands. It is imperative upon us to remember that at the end of the story, God disallows Abraham from sacrificing his son Isaac.

The book of Leviticus details the sacrifices in the holy Temple; it also helps us discover the deeper teaching of not only what it means to be a Jew, but also of what it means to be a human being.

Sin and Responsibility

> *If his sacrifice is a burnt offering of the herd, he shall offer a male without blemish; he shall bring it of his own free will to the entrance of the Tent of Meeting, before God. And he shall lay his hands upon the head of the burnt offering, and it shall then be accepted as an atonement for him.*
>
> LEVITICUS 1:3–4

*V*ayikra introduces us to the ritual requirements of sacrifice, and in doing so it asks that we probe the nature of the sin. For some liberal and liberated intellectuals, the outmoded 's' word is a relic of a puritanical society which obsessively sought to inflict guilt upon its citizenry; for other theologically-minded strict constructionists, sin is the inevitable master of the human personality, which can only be overcome by divine grace. Advocates of the first position tend to blame genes and environment – parents and society – for whatever wrongdoing is perpetuated by individual "victims"; advocates of the second view human nature as a most powerful and relentless enemy from within. Both agree that the human being himself is more object than subject, virtually defenseless in the face of the evil forces which are in control.

The Bible, on the other hand, presumes individual responsibility, and therefore one's ability to control one's actions. For a willful transgression, a sacrificial offering is not sufficient: restitution must be made, complete repentance must be effectuated, and often an additional rehabilitative penalty must be paid (*knas*). A "sin offering" comes into play only with unwitting transgression (*shogeg*) whereby, for example, a person kindles a fire on the Sabbath day either because he was unaware that such an activity was biblically forbidden, or because he was unaware that the particular day was Saturday. The very purpose of the sacrifice – the individual who brings the animal to the holy Temple must confess his sin over it before it is ritually slaughtered – may very well be to emphasize the fact that even in such an instance, human responsibility demands that a transgression has taken place, albeit of a lesser nature than a sin of wilful greed or passion. Ignorance of the law is no excuse: every normal person must be aware of his environment and of the possible ramifications of his every deed.

Ultimately, these sacrificial laws come to teach us that taking responsibility is not a choice but a necessity, and that if one accepts responsibility then one has the possibility of repenting and thereby recreating oneself, which is symbolized by the fire on the altar whose flames not only can destroy, but can also transform and purify.

In the book of Genesis, two versions of the creation of the human emerge. Chapter one emphasizes the creation of the human being in God's image, thereby commanding him to conquer the world. Chapter two, however, emphasizes the human being who emanated from the dust of the earth is even destined to serve that very earth out of which he was formed.

My rebbe and mentor, the late Rabbi Soloveitchik, in his masterpiece *The Lonely Man of Faith*, suggests that these are not two different accounts of creation, but are rather two different views of the human being. According to the mechanistic school, the human is no more than a complex animal, subject to all the laws of nature which enslave and limit the beast. Behaviorist psychology, as enunciated by Skinner's *Walden Two*, is based on this attitude, which ultimately denies real freedom of choice. The opposing vitalistic view says that in addition to the animal, the human possesses a transcendent element, a divine spark which ensures his freedom and gives him the ability to direct his own destiny.

By providing two complementary accounts of the creation of the human being, the Torah seems to be acknowledging the truth of both positions together. Indeed, the human creature is dangerously close to being thwarted by instinct and raw passion, since he possesses the brute characteristics of animals. Nonetheless, he can and must raise himself above the animal world, even above his own genetically endowed and environmentally influenced characteristics, and recreate himself. He must be held responsible for his deeds – not only for what he does, but also for what he should have done and did not do, for what he should have been aware of and was unaware.

We read in Genesis how God affirms that "it was good" after each separate act of creation – except after the final step, the sixth day, when man was created. There follows then a concluding assessment that God saw that all of His creation was good – but not necessarily the specific creation of the human being. Seforno derives a valuable teaching from this seeming discrepancy: All other creations were functional beings and their functions are judged by the Almighty to be good and necessary for the world. The human being alone is a moral being. Whether or not he chooses correctly, whether or not he realizes his potential function to help perfect and imperfect society and world, depends entirely on him – and so God cannot provide any advance judgment.

There is a moral fable about a sculptor who was seeking a model for a statue which he wanted to entitle, "Beauty–Goodness." Naturally, he was searching for the harmony of spirit and soma which would enable the purity of soul to pierce through the external form. He found the proper individual at a spirited prayer convocation, and he knew that he had not erred when his subject requested that any remuneration be given to the poor. After achieving a major success, the sculptor set out to do a companion piece, "Ugliness–Evil." He spent years searching for the right model, to no avail. Then one evening he chanced upon a drunk lying amidst his filth in a slimy gutter. Fascinated by the decadence of the face, the artist gently lifted the drunk in his arms, brought him to his studio, and worked feverishly all night in order to produce the basis for what he was certain would be his second masterpiece. The next morning, when the drunk awoke and the sculptor had him cleaned and dressed as the beginning of his payment, one can imagine his shock in discovering that here was the very same model which he had used for his previous masterpiece. Who and what was the true model? It depends on the individual at the moment of his choice – and we all have the responsibility to make the right choice at every moment.

The Modern Significance of Animal Sacrifice

*But its innards and its legs shall he wash in water
and the priest shall burn all on the altar, to be a
burnt sacrifice, an offering made by fire, of a sweet
savor unto God.*

LEVITICUS 1:9

Animals, knives, entrails, gore... the world of sacrifices is not
a particularly pleasant one to conjure up in our imagination. If we are
predisposed to thinking of such rituals as primitive and animalistic, not
fit for conversation at the dinner table, then the challenge to achieve a
modicum of understanding is even greater.

Undoubtedly, sacrifices are one of the most disturbing subjects
in the entire Torah. One branch of Jewry found it so enigmatic and
annoying that they simply swept it under the rug of forgetfulness, qui-
etly editing the prayer book so that any reference to future sacrifices
disappeared without a trace. Their synagogue Torah readings suffered
the same editing job with much of Leviticus, including the portion of
Vayikra, ending up on the cutting-room floor.

Perhaps a good way to lift our veil of prejudices is to see how the major commentators addressed the issue. In his *Guide for the Perplexed* (Part 3, Ch. 32), Maimonides takes a rational view of the issue.* Disturbed himself about the need for sacrifices, he explains that traversing from a state of mind firmly at home with the practices of idolatrous sacrifices in Egypt to the pure monotheistic worship implicit in a holy nation could not be done in one leap. Before the Israelites became the Israelites, they lived in a world where sacrifices were part of the grammar of existence, a language everyone knew and spoke intimately. To command the future Israelites to abandon completely any trace of this world could not be done. Therefore, the sacrifices are part of a weaning-away process for the children of Israel: to keep the basic form, because that spoke to their sense of awe, but change the subject matter, replacing idols with God as the focus of worship.

Several chapters ahead (Ch. 46), Maimonides points out that God specifically commanded the Israelites to sacrifice a paschal lamb for the festival of Passover. Sheep were worshiped by the Egyptians, and God wanted the Israelites to understand that He did not abide idolatry. Even if they would continue to sacrifice, the nature of their sacrifices would have to change entirely.

Nahmanides was not pleased with the Maimonidean approach, attacking his claim that sacrifices were a compromise for the unenlightened Israelites still steeped in their primitive ways. He finds it self-contradictory that if God essentially didn't want sacrifices to begin with, why would the Torah speak of sacrifices in terms of "a sweet savor unto God" (Lev. 1:9).

Nahmanides rejects Maimonides' negative approach to the subject of sacrifices, citing the Torah's own record, which never speaks of sacrifices negatively. On the contrary, when Noah emerges from the ark and offers sacrifices, we read how "…God smelled the sweet savor" (Gen. 8:21). And earlier, when Abel brought his sacrifice, arousing the jealousy of his brother Cain, the Torah tells us that "God had respect to Abel and his offering" (Gen. 4:4).

---

*   For further treatment of Maimonides' position, see chapter 10.

After his defense of the Torah's positive attitude toward the institution of sacrifices, Nahmanides goes on to explore a deeper level:

> Since actions of human beings involved thought, speech and action, God commanded that when a person sins he must bring a sacrifice, his hands leaning on the animal, corresponding to the action. And he shall confess with his mouth, corresponding to speech, and he shall burn the innards and the kidneys, which are the source of thought and lust ... And he shall pour the blood on the altar, thinking that he himself is worthy of having his own blood spilled and his body burned were it not for the lovingkindness of God who has taken a substitute for him, the sacrifice atoning for him, its blood for his blood, its life-force for his life-force.
>
> Nachmanides on Leviticus 1:9

In dividing the elements of the sacrifice into thought, word and action, Nahmanides is not merely giving us a categorical structure of the event, but is also alluding to the powerful linkage – and even identity – between the sinner and the sacrifice. The hand that leans on the animal about to be slaughtered, the mouth that confesses, the fire that burns out those organs which correspond to our thoughts, make us realize that sacrifice is not for anyone's sake but ourselves. *We* must be moved by the sacrifices, and not *God*; God will only be moved by our movement, our realization of wrong-doing and achievement of repentance. And lest we mistakenly believe that the idea of "sweet savor" necessarily posits a God in need of the scent of our sacrifices, Nahmanides reminds us what the Talmud declares: "Would anyone think that God requires food, He owns the world and all of its fullness!" (*Menaḥot* 110a).

Clearly then, the sacrifices are for our sake, and for the sake of change, the most important and most difficult goal a person can have: self-awareness and self-understanding which lead to an existential personality change, resulting in a different and improved individual. Since true repentance is so difficult to achieve, it requires a traumatic jolt. The person who recognizes the fundamental truth – that he was granted life in return for commitment to fulfill the Torah's commands and that, if he has fallen short of his responsibility he is the one who deserves to be sacrificed on the altar – could not possibly remain complacent and apathetic when he sees the fire lick the flesh of the animal, when he sees the blood of the animal sprinkled on the altar, when he himself makes his confession over an animal about to die. The horror and and shock and terror he feels as the animal goes up in flames should provide him with the strength and conviction and resolution to change his ways. Just as he sinned with thought, words and action, he must now realize that "thinking" of change and "speaking" of change is not enough. He must act. He must change. He must transform himself. He must emerge from the sacrifice as a new individual, worthy of a renewed lease on life.

Rabbi Yaakov Mecklenburg, in his commentary *Haktav V'Hakabbalah*, also discusses sacrifices in terms of changing the individual, and his starting point is precisely the phrase "sweet savor" emphasized by Nahmanides. Not only is it an evocative metaphor for attributing something uniquely indefinable to the idea of sacrifices, but the words "sweet savor" are to instruct the person bringing the sacrifice not to make the mistake of believing that his job is done and his sin is forgiven immediately upon the sprinkling of the animal's blood. Sin will be forgiven only if the sacrifice works on the person offering the sacrifice by making him into a different person. The sacrifice must change the individual's heart and ways. The fulfillment of the ritual must be accompanied with repentance, a profound change of personality. That's why it's called "sweet savor," says Rabbi Mecklenberg. When a person puts on sweet-smelling perfume, we smell the perfume before we even see the person and it leaves its unmistakable trace even after he has disappeared from view. In this sense, sacrifice is a "perfume of sweet savor unto God," heralding to God that a new individual is now in the process of being formed and that he will continue to be scented sweetly even after he has left the particular place where he made his sacrifice. Only if that happens, if the event of the sacrifice itself affects the Israelite both before and after, will his sacrifice effectuate divine forgiveness.

Does Judaism Believe in Democracy?

If the entire congregation of Israel shall err through ignorance, and the thing be hidden from the eyes of the assembly and they have done something against any of the commandments of the Lord concerning things which should not be done and have incurred guilt; when the sin which they have sinned is known, then the assembly shall offer a young bullock for the sin and bring it before the Tent of Meeting.

LEVITICUS 4:13-14

To what extent, if at all, does our rabbinic tradition believe in democracy – the rule of the people? Most religionists would assume that Judaism must believe in theocracy, the rule of the divine. But how can we possibly arrive at the divine will if God is no longer clearly enunciating the decisions regarding the political and military questions at hand, neither in the form of a commanding voice heard by all as in the revelation at Sinai nor even in the emergence of prophets who preach in His name?

We don't even have an operating body of religio-legal leadership – such as a *sanhedrin* (Jewish Court of seventy-one rabbinic judges) – which could lay claim to the right of governance under the banner of nomocracy or "Toracracy/halakhacracy" – the rule of the law rooted in revelation and tradition. Where must serious and well-meaning Israeli Jews go for authoritative decisions, given the wide range and sharp divergence of opinions among both rabbinic leaders and military spokespeople!?

I believe that a careful study of our foremost theologian-jurist-philosopher Maimonides will prove conclusively that we do look to the will of the majority of our citizenry for guidance, and that the source for Maimonides' belief in democracy is a verse in this week's biblical reading.

Maimonides, unlike most other Talmudic commentaries and codifiers, deals with many critical matters of governance, especially but not exclusively in his "Laws of Kings" (chapters 11, 12). The very first mishna in the Tractate *Sanhedrin* ordains that the bestowal of rabbinic ordination (*semikha*) is effectuated by three sages; this *semikha* (literally, the laying of the hands of the elder sage upon the shoulders of the younger scholar as a symbol of passing over the tradition) harks back to God's emanation of a portion of His divine spirit upon Moses, who then ordained the elders. This chain of Jewish leadership came to a tragic end in the third century under Roman rule, when the decree was made that anyone who bestowed ordination and anyone who received ordination would be killed (*Sanhedrin* 13b, 14a).

Maimonides, in his *Interpretation to the Mishna*, writes as follows:

> It seems to me that when there will be agreement from all the sages of Jerusalem and their disciples* to raise up someone to precede them [in greatness] and make him their leader, and on the condition that this is in the land of Israel, this agreed-upon person shall be the central pillar of the Academy and shall become ordained; afterwards, he will ordain whomever he deems worthy.

In accordance with accepted rules of Talmudic law, the agreement need

---

* In his interpretation of the Mishna in *Bekhorot* 29b Maimonides writes: "agreement by all the residents of the land of Israel."

not be unanimous; a majority is always considered as though it were a unanimous decision (*"rubo kekulo"*).

In effect, therefore, Maimonides has ruled that the biblical – and divinely originated – ordination, which empowered our Judges to innovate decrees and boldly interpret Jewish law, could be resuscitated by a majority vote of the populace in Israel.

The rationale for Maimonides' novel position is clearly exposited in his commentary:

> If you do not take such a stand [for such a democratic vote], a Great Sanhedrin will never again exist, since the members of such a court must be ordained. And the Holy One Blessed be He testifies that the Sanhedrin will be restored, as it is written: "And I shall restore your Judges as they were originally and your legal advisers as they were in the beginning; only afterwards can [Jerusalem] be called the City of Righteousness."
>
> Isaiah 1:26

The necessity for such a democratic procedure is clear to Maimonides, because he insisted that the messianic era – replete with a reinstated and fully improvised Sanhedrin and a city of Jerusalem featuring the third Temple – must come about through *natural,* and not supernatural, means. And indeed, such a democratic procedure was instituted in sixteenth-century Safed, when Rabbi Yaakov bei Rav was "elected" Head of the Academy, and he ordained a number of outstanding scholarly pietists, foremost among them being Rabbi Yosef Karo. (Unfortunately, the nascent Sanhedrin was short-lived due to the opposition of Jerusalem scholars, led by Rabbi Levi Ibn Haviv, who felt overlooked by their Safed brethren).

I believe that the textual basis for Maimonides' far-reaching decision is a verse in this biblical portion. It must be remembered that Judaism has never entertained any kind of "papal" infallibility; our Bible records that even Moses himself sinned by striking the rock, and our High Priest began the movingly dramatic Yom Kippur Temple service by publicly requesting from God forgiveness for his personal transgressions. The book of Leviticus teaches:

If the entire congregation of Israel shall err, and a matter [of
proper conduct] become obscured from the eyes of the assembly...and they become guilty...the assembly shall offer a young
bull as a sin offering...

Leviticus 4:13, 14

Our sages query how the entire nation can commit an unwitting transgression, and conclude that it must be the result of a mistaken ruling
which emerged from the Sanhedrin, to permit that which ought to have
been prohibited; this conclusion demands that the biblical phrase "entire
congregation of Israel" (*adat* Yisrael) must mean the Sanhedrin (*Torat
Kohanim* 4, 241; *Horayot* 6b). If, then, the Great Sanhedrin is biblically
equated with the congregation of Israel, the way of re-instituting the
ordination which is necessary in the formation of the Sanhedrin must
be by agreement of a majority of the nation; the congregation of Israel
is also defined by the sages of the Talmud as referring to the Congregation of Jews living in Israel (*Horayot* 3b).

On this basis, it becomes almost obvious why Maimonides fur-
ther rules that in the absence of Sanhedrin or prophet, it is the people
who must elect the king or prime minister of Israel (Interpretation of the
Mishna, *Kritut* 1:1); the sixteenth-century authority Rabbenu David b.
Zimra agrees with this position (Commentary to Maimonides, Laws of
Kings 3:8), and so did the first Chief Rabbi of Israel, Rabbi A.I. Hakohen
Kook, who declares that all the laws ascribed to a king of Israel apply
to such an elected prime minister (*Mishpat Kohen*, Responsum 144, 15,
1). Indeed, our biblical source which equates the Sanhedrin with the
congregation of Israel would seem to confirm that in the absence of a
Sanhedrin, the national opinion – by referendum or election – should
be considered authoritative.

Hence, it is no wonder that throughout the Middle Ages, the Jewish communities – both in Europe and the Orient – were run in a purely
democratic fashion in accordance with the decisions of the Seven Good
Councilmen chosen by popular election. Such a procedure was ordained
by the *Hoshen Mishpat* – as long as the decisions of the Council were
not in opposition to absolute Torah law. This fundamental acceptance
of government for and by the majority of the people – as well as the

Jewish principle of human freedom which emanates from the biblical axiom of all human beings having been created by God in His image and underscored by our divinely-aided freedom from Egyptian bondage – made Judaism the model for the democratic governance established by the founding fathers of the United States of America as well as of the modern State of Israel.

The Truest and the Hardest Sacrifice:
Admission of Guilt

When a ruler will have sinned...

LEVITICUS 4:24

During their sojourn in the wilderness, the Almighty instructs Moses to inform the Israelites about the right of repentance for committing a sin:

> If anyone is guilty of transgression...he must confess the sin which he committed.
>
> Numbers 5:7

Maimonides makes this commandment the hallmark of his Laws of Repentance (1:1), codifying that the command to repent must begin with a confession of guilt spoken directly and personally to the individual who was wronged (if it is an interpersonal sin), or to God if it is a ritual transgression. Above all, the person must verbalize his guilt to

37

himself. If admission of guilt were not so difficult, it would not count as the very definition of repentance.

In biblical times, in addition to confession the individual who transgressed would also bring special sin offerings, but a sin offering without individual heartfelt repentance was not only meaningless but was considered by God an abomination (Is. 1:10–15).

In this portion of *Vayikra*, the Bible first sets the stage by informing us that human beings will of necessity sin, "A soul, when it will unwittingly sin..." (Lev. 4:2). And who is the very first sinner to be singled out? No lesser individual than the High Priest himself, the most exalted religious personality in Israel, the guardian of the holy Temple.

Apparently our Bible does not recognize one scintilla of "papal infallibility"; the Bible even emphasizes that "if the High Priest will sin, it is a transgression upon the whole nation," a sacrilegious blotch on our national escutcheon (Lev. 4:3, Rashi ad loc.). And on the great white fast of the day of forgiveness, the first individual to confess his guilt and request purification is the High Priest. Indeed, the first word to escape the mouth of our most sacred and exalted human being on the most sacred and exalted day of the year is *"Ana,"* please, oh woe, a cry of personal and human anguish.

The next in line for sinning and admission of guilt is the Sanhedrin, the highest court in the land, the keepers of the divine law. When the lawmakers sin in judgment, all of Israel automatically sins, because they – the judges – are entrusted with seeing that justice is done throughout society. The elders of the congregation as well as the High Priest must share in the guilt of the Sanhedrin, because they should have prevented the travesty of an unfit judiciary (Lev. 4:13, 15, 16).

And the third who is singled out, who must confess and atone, is the prince (*nasi*), the ruler, the president, the prime minister. Amazingly, whereas the Bible uses the word "if" (*im*) regarding the transgression of the High Priest and the Sanhedrin, it uses the word "when" (*asher*) regarding the *nasi*. Why is the number-one wielder of power most likely to fall prey to sin? Is it because he comes to believe he is above the law, that what is good for him is automatically good for the State? Is it because he must rely on popular support, so he may fall prey to giving the people not what they need but what they want, to acting not in accordance with what is right but in accordance with the latest opinion poll.* The Bible doesn't quite tell us, but it does say that he is most vulnerable.

King Saul didn't wait for Samuel the Judge to begin the public sacrifice, and lost the kingdom (1 Sam. 1:13). King David committed adultery and sent Bathsheba's husband to the front lines of battle to die, and remained the progenitor of the Davidic dynasty (11 Sam., 12). Why? Because Saul attempted to justify himself and blame the nation, whereas King David admitted his guilt and wept before the prophet and God.

Rashi (Lev. 4:22) links the Hebrew "*asher*" ("when" the *nasi* sins) to the Hebrew "*ashrei*," fortunate: "fortunate is the generation whose *nasi* puts his heart and mind toward seeking forgiveness for his sins."

Apparently, the very first sacrifice the sinner must bring is his own ego, his own self-image. This sacrifice is much more difficult than any animal or meal offering; it is the admission of guilt of the individual which must be the first step in repentance and the achievement of forgiveness.

---

* See *Meshekh Ḥokhma*, ad loc.

Prayers – Not Supplication, but Sacrifice

Hear our prayer, O Lord Our God...

FROM THE AMIDA PRAYER

Prayer seems to be a rather egoistic and presumptuous experience. After all, most people pray when something goes wrong, not when something goes right and they seem to be making demands or at least requests of the divine! Indeed, if we hear someone who never seemed particularly religious declare, "I went to pray yesterday," our immediate reaction would be: "Why, what's wrong?" The very English word "prayer" (an imprecise translation of the ambiguous Hebrew *tefilla*) means petition.

Prayer, one of the most basic of human concerns, is really quite elusive. On the surface it seems relatively simple, especially if one relies upon the popular image of a bowed head, eyes filled with tears as lips silently request a reprieve from a fatal illness – or any number of tragic circumstances that periodically sunder peaceful lives with their maddening urgency.

But classical Jewish prayer is not solely based on the specific needs of an individual at a given moment. Of course there is room for personal requests before the Almighty, but these are not the primary focus of Jewish prayer according to many of our greatest sages. The Talmud discusses the genesis of the three obligatory prayer "services" each day – morning, afternoon and night (*Berakhot* 26b). One view maintains that the three daily prayers correspond to the prayers which each of the patriarchs established: Abraham, the morning (*shaḥarit*), Isaac, the afternoon (*minḥa*), and Jacob, the night prayer (*ma'ariv*). The other view insists that our prayers correspond to the daily communal sacrifices, the subject of the portion of *Vayikra*. After the completion and the consecration of the Sanctuary that ends the book of Exodus, the book of Leviticus opens with the entire sacrificial rite that would later become the major part of the service in the holy Temple. The Talmudic discussion concludes by linking our times for obligatory prayer to the times of the obligatory daily communal sacrifices – and this connection will teach us a great deal about the unique Jewish attitude toward prayer in general.

In addition to the sacrifices individuals might bring as a result of spontaneously induced "gifts" to the Almighty and his priest-teachers, daily communal sacrifices were also required in the morning *tamid* sacrifice, the afternoon *tamid* sacrifice and night incense offering emanating from burning the leftovers. Linking prayer with sacrifice immediately causes us to change focus; instead of petitioning God to fulfill our request, we are obligated to bring an offering to Him. Instead of asking what God can do for us, we must consider what we can do for Him. And what is the most meaningful gift we can give the Almighty? Ourselves! So first and foremost in prayer we commit ourselves to God, creating a far more mature, unselfish and significant relationship than would occur if our primary connection to the One Above focused on what He will do for us. Even in Temple times, the communal sacrifices were accompanied by prayers.[*]

Second, linking prayer to daily sacrifice emphasizes the primary element of service intrinsic to prayer, an "I serve You'" rather than an "I need You" relationship. Maimonides (Laws of Prayer 1:1) rules that we must pray daily, citing the verse "And you shall serve the Lord your

---

[*] See essay "Uplifting the World," (p.13). See, for example, Mishna *Tamid* 5:1 and 7:2.

God" (Ex. 23:25) and then illustrating that service (*avoda*) need not be limited to the Temple altar but can also be of the human heart, as in the biblical verse which we recite in the *Shema*, "...and you shall serve Him with all your heart" (Deut. 11:13).

The essential thrust for daily service of the heart begins with the realization that God owes me nothing but I owe Him everything for having given me life; prayer moves humans toward a basic joyous acceptance of one's place in the universe.

Service of the heart is thanksgiving for waking up to another day and trains the Jew to value what he has been given. It is not petitioning for what I feel I need and even perhaps deserve, but it is thanksgiving for what I have already received. It is not future oriented, it is past oriented. God deserves my service if only because He has given me the gift and challenge of life – and I dare not take that for granted. This "service" definition of prayer will hopefully teach me to live my life thankful for what I have rather than frustrated for what I lack. A most beloved elementary-school principal of mine, Rabbi Menachem Mandel, of blessed memory, once asked us who was wealthier, the man with $100 or the man with $200. We immediately answered the man with $200. "Wrong," he said, "You must measure an individual's wealth not by what he has, but rather by what he believes he lacks." And since it is the nature of the world that most people wish to double what they have, since the individual with $100 feels he is lacking half of what the individual with $200 lacks, the one with $100 is wealthier than the one with $200.

Third, prayer is usually thought of as a personal and individual expression of an objective and individual need. Not so with Jewish prayer. Since the daily sacrifices in the Temple were financed by the yearly half-shekel given by every Jew at the beginning of the month of Adar, the communal offerings were brought in the name of all of Israel (*korban tsibur*). Sacrifice-based prayer is a much more communal and national experience. For that reason, our statutory prayer (*Amida*) is always in the plural: "Heal us, O God so that we may be healed," and "Hear our prayer, O Lord Our God." Not only does our prayer link us to the entire Jewish community throughout the world, but it also joins our aspirations to the dreams and hopes of historic Israel, throughout the generations: "Return us, O God, to Your Torah...Look upon our travail and plead our cause…to Jerusalem Your city may You return through compassion…May you cause the plant of David your servant to grow speedily…."

Jewish prayer brings comfort not because it guarantees immediate response, like putting three dollars into a sandwich machine and out comes a tuna-on-roll, but rather because it makes the Israelite feel part of a historic nation which is much greater than he/she is as an individual, because it nurtures an attitude which uplifts the single person to look beyond his/her own specific needs and desires and join together into the vision and mission of a historic nation. It also reminds the individual that despite difficult and even destructive past events, that nation has managed to endure, survive and even prevail.

Superficially, submerging my own desires to the desires of the Jewish nation may seem limiting, but in reality this experience of prayer is most expanding and liberating. It removes the focus from someone who must eventually die and disappear, and with him all his private designs and personal dreams, and shifts it to the larger and eternal reality of the Jewish nation and redemption. *Reb Yisrael* is transient and is ultimately owed nothing; *Am Yisrael* is eternal and has the divine guarantee of redemption. Only insofar as the individual has the capacity to submerge himself and dedicate his life to his nation will he overcome his existential frustrations and transcend his personal mortality. From this perspective, "we" prayer enables the individual to transcend his transient existence and participate in Israel's eternity.

The Talmud records the following incident:

> A disciple once went before the ark [to serve as cantor] in the presence of Rabbi Eliezer and was especially lengthy in his prayers. The congregation complained. Rabbi Eliezer responded: Was he more lengthy than Moses our Teacher, whose prayer lasted for forty days and forty nights? Another time another disciple went before the ark [to serve as cantor] in the presence of Rabbi Eliezer and was especially brief in his prayers. The congregation complained. Rabbi Eliezer responded: Was he briefer than Moses our Teacher, who prayed, "God, please heal her now."
>
> *Berakhot* 34a

When Moses prayed for all of Israel after their sin with the golden calf, he came before God with the strength of the divine covenantal promise of Jewish eternity, and so he prayed at great length, with even a righteous demand. But when Moses makes a personal petition for his sister Miriam, on behalf of whom God never gave a guarantee, he merely allows himself five words, as a poor beggar at the gates of the wealthy householder, with neither claim nor power.

Personal, selfish prayer is a natural and understandable, individual need; communal sacrificial prayer is a natural, and even eternal, gift to the divine.

Tzav

Maimonides on Sacrifices, Revisited

> *And the Lord spoke to Moses saying: 'Command*
> *Aaron and his sons, saying, this is the law of the*
> *burnt offering...'*
>
> LEVITICUS 6:1–2

When first encountering the concept of animal sacrifices in the book of Leviticus,* we explored in depth the views of Maimonides and Nahmanides. Maimonides, in his classic work, *Guide for the Perplexed*, explained that the purpose of these sacrifices was in order to distance the Jewish people from idolatry.

After all, having just emerged from Egypt, it was natural that their spirits remained chained to an idolatrous system of sacrificial worship. Hence Maimonides argues that the Israelites were so accustomed to the practice of animal sacrifices and the burning of incense that when the time arrived to create a new model of worship, out of necessity God based it on the Egyptian system which they had known.

---

* See essay "Uplifting the World," (p. 13).

Because it is impossible to move suddenly from one extreme to the other.... divine wisdom ... could not command that [the Israelites] leave all of those ways of worship, depart from them and nullify them. For such [a demand] would have been something that no human mind could expect, given the nature of the human being who is always drawn to that to which he is accustomed." Therefore God retained the sacrificial acts, but transformed them into means rather than ends, declaring that they must become the implements for directing all such energies and activities into the worship of the one true God of the Universe.

Guide for the Perplexed, Part III, Chap. 32

Perhaps another way of interpreting the Maimonidean position can be extracted from a striking Talmudic passage in Tractate *Yoma*. There we are told how the Jewish people complain to the Almighty that the inclination of idolatry has destroyed the Temple, burned down the Sanctuary, killed all the righteous, exiled the Israelites from their land, and – to add insult to injury – "... it is still dancing amongst us." They request that it be vanquished. The Almighty accedes to their desire, and after a fast of three days and three nights, God allows them to destroy the evil inclination towards idolatry. And what is the object they destroyed? "He came forth in the image of a lion of fire emerging from the Holy of Holies" (*Yoma* 69b).

What a strange description for the evil inclination of idolatry, "a lion of fire emerging from the Holy of Holies!" The famous interpreter of *Aggadot* (Talmudic legends) Rabbi Shmuel Eidels (1555–1631), known as the Maharsha, apparently troubled by what appears to be such a positive image of evil idolatry, explains that this refers to the zodiac sign Leo (the lion), which rules the heavens during Av (August) when the holy Temple was destroyed. And indeed, the first Temple was destroyed largely because of the idolatrous practices of the Israelites.

The Hassidic master Rabbi Zadok Hakohen of Lublin is likewise surprised by the Talmudic description. After all, the lion is a most respected Jewish symbol, representing the majesty of Judah who is thrice identified with a lion in Jacob's blessings:

50

Judah is a lion's whelp; from the prey, my son, thou art gone up.
He stooped down, he crouched as a lion, and as a lioness; who
shall raise him?

Genesis 49:9

The lion is also an aspect of the divine *merkava* (chariot) in the vision of
Ezekiel, and is generally depicted on the ark curtains (*parokhet*) guarding the Torah. Moreover, the Holy of Holies would hardly be a proper
home for the evil inclination of idolatry.

And so he suggests that the message of the Talmudic passage is
that every aspect of creation – including idolatry – has its roots in sanctity. When we reflect upon the various gods of the ancient world – the
Sun and the Moon, Herculean strength, Zeusian power and Aphrodi-
tian beauty – they are all aspects of the physical world and the instinctive drives which are fundamental to the world around us even today.

One response to these physical and human drives is the ascetic
option, denigrating and attempting to root out all physicality because
of the dangers which can follow from uncontrolled addiction to their
urges. This, however, has never been the Jewish response.

After all, the Almighty did not create us as disembodied spirits
or ethereal intellects. The physical side of our beings must have value
if it was created by God. The challenge is to direct – or sublimate – our
instinctive drives properly, to see them as means and not ends, not to
deny them but to ennoble them, and to utilize them in the service of
the divine. This may well be the true meaning of Maimonides' words.

When the Jews left Egypt, they still carried with them the imprint
of Egyptian idolatries, the myriad of gods including manifestations of
nature (the sun) and beasts, which they held up as ideals. According
to Maimonides, Leviticus is the history of how God redirected these
idolatrous energies, teaching the Jews to build a Sanctuary as a means
toward divine service, to sanctify sexual energy within the context of
marriage and family, to utilize strength and power in order to recreate
society in the divine kingship.

The fact of the matter is that what was true at the time when the
Jews left Egypt has not necessarily changed to this day, and quite likely

may never change. And therefore the Maimonidean position regarding the animal sacrifices – to wean the Israelites away from their previous Egyptian passions – is not a temporary solution for a particular generation; we are still in need of the directed discipline which will enable us to direct and ennoble our drives and passions to the service of the God of compassion and justice.

Textual evidence for this can be found at the end of the Talmudic passage we quoted earlier. The prophet cleverly warns the Israelites, after the evil instinct was given over into their hands: "Remember, if you kill him, the world will be destroyed" (*Ibid*). And so we read how they imprisoned the evil desire, and after three days not one egg could be found in the Land of Israel; apparently, without the sexual attraction between male and female, creation cannot exist. Indeed, the evil instinct is a "lion of fire" which can destroy or purify, depending upon how this natural force is utilized.

It may very well be that what Maimonides understood about the generation which left Egypt may turn out to be an eternal law of human nature: Our passions are not to be destroyed but are to be directed, are not to be consumed but are to be consecrated.

Of Sinners and Saints

> And the Lord spoke to Moses saying: 'Speak to
> Aaron and his sons, saying this is the law of the
> sin offering: At the very same place where the
> whole burnt offering shall be slaughtered, there
> shall the sin offering be slaughtered before the
> Lord; it is the Holy of the Holy.
>
> LEVITICUS 6:17, 18

It seems rather strange that the "whole burnt offering" which represents total dedication to God and is the highest expression of complete commitment, is to be offered in the very same place where the transgressor brings his sin offering. Would it not have been more logical for there to have been two separate places for these two very separate types of sacrifices? Remember that the very first whole burnt offering was the lamb which father Abraham brought as a substitute for Isaac, the lamb which has become for all time the symbol of consummate dedication to God. So why mix and match two such different individuals on two such different ends of the religious spectrum? And why does our biblical verse conclude with the words "Holy of the Holy," which seems to refer not only to the whole burnt offering but also to the sin offering?

My first response would be that that is precisely the point that our Bible is trying to make, a Bible which is anxious to preserve the anonymity of the sinners, who must express their sin to God but not necessarily to anyone else. Once the sinner brings his sin offering to the very same place that the dedicated individual brings his whole burnt offering, no onlooker could ever condemn an individual because he saw him or her offering a sacrifice in a particular place within the Temple precinct.

In addition, the Torah is teaching us about the range of the human personality. One day you're a vice president and the next day you're typing as an office temp, scrounging to make a dollar. One day you're holy, *kadosh*, and the next day you're mired in unscrupulous behavior. The individual bringing the sin offering today might well bring a burnt offering tomorrow!

Last, the sin offering and the burnt offering are brought in the same spot because in essence they're not that far apart. It was the sweet Psalmist King David who taught, "From the depths do I call out to thee, O God" (Ps. 130:1). It is only when an individual descends to rock bottom that he realizes the necessity of a divine anchor. Sin can often lead to salvation. The Baal Shem Tov taught that the seed must first rot in the ground before it can begin to flower.

Shortly after my aliyah, when attempting to learn about Israeli society, I gave a lecture at an Israeli prison with nearly four hundred incarcerated men. On the evening of the lecture, I found out my competition was a "shoot 'em up" action-packed cowboy and Indian John Wayne movie. Perhaps fifty inmates were at the cinema while more than two hundred who came to hear the rabbi.

Where does a rabbi turn in search of a subject when he's placed in front of an audience he never dreamed would want to hear a Torah talk? The answer, of course, is the portion of the week, and since that week happened to be *Shemot*, naturally I scoured my memory for things to say about the children of Jacob in exile. But someone interrupted me and asked if I'd mind speaking about the previous week's reading, *Vayeḥi*. When I asked why, he explained that they loved to hear about Joseph, since Joseph had also been in prison and had been freed! Indeed, it had been in anticipation of hearing about Joseph that so many inmates had come to a Bible lecture instead of a movie about the Wild West.

Some of the prisoners had sauntered in bareheaded, very tough-looking in their tight jeans and polo shirts which emphasized muscle more than anything else, while others wore yarmulkes and tzitzit tucked outside their pants. The contrast was stark, but the intensity of involvement came from all camps. It was an amazing audience, unlike anything I'd ever experienced before.

After the class, we davened *ma'ariv*, the evening prayer, and I must confess that I hadn't been so moved since last Yom Kippur, and this was just an ordinary week night. I realized that in jail, every day must have an element of Yom Kippur, where sin and punishment are one's daily fare.

The man leading the prayers was a Sephardi Jew who said the words with fear and trembling, his lips enunciating each syllable as if he were carving stone with his teeth. The davening must have taken more than half an hour, three times the usual length. Afterwards, I asked him where he derived his power of prayer and concentration. He told me the following story.

One day he came home unexpectedly and found his wife in bed with his best friend – with their two-month-old baby daughter between them. Since he was employed as a guard, he always carried a gun. He couldn't control his angry passion and meant to shoot at his friend, but actually killed his own child. Now he was sentenced to life imprisonment. He descended into a deep depression and even attempted an unsuccessful suicide. His wife left him, his parents wouldn't even visit him. And then a visiting rabbi (a Moroccan *ḥakham*) lifted him out of it. The rabbi told him two things: First, he said, apparently you made a mess of this world. But this world is only temporary; the next world is of the spirit, is timeless. This world is really a preparatory vestibule for the ultimate living room of eternal life. And what better place for one's preparation than a prison devoid of many temptations which only cause the individual to fall into an abyss of impurity?

Second, he had felt totally isolated and alone with no one coming to visit him. After all, he had killed his baby! So the *ḥakham* further explained that one of God's descriptive names is *Raḥum*, literally "Compassionate One," a term which comes from the Hebrew word *reḥem*, womb. What is the connection? A mother has no difficulty diapering her baby, accepting the one who emanated from her womb with all of its dirt. After all, the baby is an inextricable part of her – and we each accept ourselves! The mother even kisses the baby as she diapers it. So does the Almighty accept all of His children wherever they may be – physically and spiritually. God will always come to visit you; He will embrace and kiss you, no matter what you have done. He is the God of unconditional love, both and before after you sin. You must only let Him in…!

I came to jail during the week of *Shemot* and ended up speaking about *Vayeḥi*, but what I received from the prisoner was an insight into *Tzav*: How a prisoner's sin offering can help him feel the deep anguish he should feel about the crime he committed, but also how that very sin offering can lead to a whole new perspective about God and the world which can literally turn sinner into saint.

Perhaps this is what our sages mean when they teach: "Where the penitent stands even the most righteous cannot stand" (*Berakhot* 34b).

Deeds and Thoughts: In Ethics It's the Deed That Counts; In Ritual, It's the Thought That Counts

> *If any of the flesh of the sacrifice of his peace offering should be eaten at all on the third day, it shall not be accepted... it shall be an abomination (pigul), and the soul that eats it shall bear his iniquity.*
>
> LEVITICUS 7:18

It has often been said that if an individual was to be incarcerated for his evil thoughts, no one would be living outside a penitentiary. Jewish law* strongly corroborates this piece of conventional wisdom:

Thoughts or emotions (*devarim shebalev*) are not of significance

---

* For example, see *Nedarim* 28a and *Kiddushin* 49b-50a.

since only a person's actions and not his/her fanciful imaginings create culpability.

However the Torah reading of *Tzav*, continuing our journey into the remote world of ritual sacrifices, specifies an exception to this common-sense rule of the paramount importance of accomplished deed over intentional desire.

According to the biblical command, the meat of the peace offering must be eaten on the same day the sacrifice is brought. When the peace offering is brought to fulfill a vow, then the time period for eating it is extended to the next day, but not to the day after that. Therefore,

> "…if any of the flesh of the sacrifice of his peace offering should be eaten at all on the third day, it shall not be accepted…it shall be an abomination (*pigul*), and the soul that eats it shall bear his iniquity."
>
> Leviticus 7:18

Rashi's comment (7:18) based on the Talmudic interpretation (*Kritut* 5a) expands the waves of the *pigul* effect to include thought as well as action; not only is it forbidden to eat a peace offering on the third day, but merely thinking, at the time of the sacrifice, that one will eat it past the proper time disqualifies that particular offering.

And since our prayers are linked to the sacrificial ritual – one view in the Talmud maintains that the three statutory prayers we recite each day correspond to the morning and afternoon sacrifices and the evening incense (*Berakhot* 26a) – it is no wonder that almost all of our sages insist that improper thoughts or even a lack of internal devotion will disqualify the prayer, no matter how carefully the words may be articulated. Why are prayers and sacrifices so inextricably bound up with the thoughts of the individual – whereas in the case of other commandments, the rule of thumb is that "divine ordinances do not require internal intent (*kavana*)…"?!

Perhaps the answer to the question can be found in the *Midrash Raba* (*Ḥukat* 8) which reports how a pagan once queried the great sage

Rabban Yohanan Ben Zakai about the paradoxical, illogical nature of the biblical commandment of the red heifer – the special, additional portion which is also read in *Tzav* – arguing that it resembled sorcery:

> You bring a cow, and burn it and grind it up and then take the ashes; if an individual has been defiled by death, you then sprinkle two or three drops on him and you declare him pure! And what is even stranger, while the ashes of this red heifer purify the impure, another pure individual who touches those ashes becomes defiled by them!
>
> *Bemidbar Raba* 19:18

The great sage responded as follows:

> "By your lives. It's not death which defiles and it's not water which purifies. It is rather the Holy One Blessed be He who declares 'I made my statutes, I have decreed my decrees.'"

Now, I believe that Rabban Yohanan Ben Zakai is saying something far more profound than merely expressing the arbitrary nature of the commandments.

Let us look at another midrashic commentary, and a fascinating insight will hopefully emerge.

> There were three things over which the Israelites protested, because they brought suffering and tribulation: the incense, the holy ark and the staff. The incense is an instrument of tribulation, because it caused the death of Nadav and Avihu (Lev. 10:2); therefore God informed Israel that it is also an instrument of atonement on the day of forgiveness. The holy ark is an instrument of tribulation, because when Uzzah touched it he was immediately struck down (II Samuel 6:7); therefore, God informed Israel that it is also an instrument of blessing of Oved Edom the Gittite (with which our enemies may be vanquished). The staff is an instrument of tribulation, because it brought the plagues upon

Egypt; therefore God informed Israel that it is also an instrument of blessing when Moses did miracles with it…

Midrash Tanḥuma, Beshallaḥ

In effect, the midrash is explaining that objects – staffs, incense, a holy ark, sacrifices, words of prayer – are not necessarily sacred in themselves. Their purpose is to bring one closer to God – and, in order for this purpose to be realized, the individual must wholeheartedly utilize them to bring him/her closer to God. As far as ritual objects are concerned, *it is not the object which is intrinsically holy, but it is rather what one does with it* and *how one relates to it in thought and intent* that creates the holiness. Therefore, the very same ashes of the red heifer can purify or defile, just as the very same holy ark can bring death or blessing, depending on the purpose for which it is utilized.

That is as far as ritual objects are concerned, but the situation is radically different concerning ethical actions. When an individual gives charity, or extends a loan to a person in need, the intent of the donor is of little or no account; his action is intrinsically significant, no matter the motivation. Hence, the Talmud rules that:

> a person who says 'I am giving a sum of money to charity so that my son may live' is still considered a completely righteous individual, a *zaddik gamur.*
>
> *Pesaḥim* 8a

Jewish theology is teaching a critical lesson here. The goal of Judaism is ethical and moral action, to walk in God's ways: Just as he is compassionate, so must we be compassionate, etc. Acts of compassion are intrinsically sacred; they are the very purpose of our being. The purpose of ritual, on the other hand, is in order to bring us close to the God of compassion, a means to an end. "You shall build me a Sanctuary, *in order that I may dwell in your midst*" (Ex. 25:8) commands God. Therefore, only rituals which are accompanied by proper intent will lead to the desired end and will therefore have eternal significance.

What Does God Really Want of Us?

> *And you shall abide at the door of the Tent of*
> *Meeting day and night for seven days and keep*
> *the charge of the Lord that you die not: for so I*
> *am commanded. So Aaron and his sons did all*
> *the things which the Lord had commanded by the*
> *hand of Moses.*
>
> LEVITICUS 8:35–36

What is the fundamental biblical definition of proper service of the Almighty? To what extent is the sacrificial cult a critical part of Jewish divine service, and where do we place the sacrifices in our hierarchy of expressions of religious devotion?

Together with the Torah portion of *Tzav*, our sages have chosen the reading of the Prophets from Jeremiah 7. What is so striking is that this biblical portion deals with the most fundamental sacrifices, both obligatory or voluntary, which the Israelites are to bring: the daily offerings, the various sin offerings and the different gift offerings. The prophetic reading opens with the glaring indictment:

> Thus says the Lord of Hosts the God of Israel: "Cease your whole burnt offerings together with your sacrifices and eat (regular) meat. This is because I did not speak to your ancestors and I did not command them on the day that I took them out from the Land of Egypt concerning issues of offerings and sacrifices."
>
> Jeremiah 7:21, 22

It is almost as though our sages are warning us against too great an involvement in the ritual of sacrifices which may lead to a depreciation of ethical and moral activities as the cornerstone of divine service. Indeed, the prophetic reading continues: "But it was this matter that I commanded them saying, 'Listen to My voice and I shall be your God and you shall be My nation'" (ibid 7:23).

The message becomes even clearer when we attempt to discover precisely which voice or which words of God the prophet is urging the Israelites to obey. Professor Yeshayahu Leibowitz discovers the proper interpretation by directing us to a later chapter in the prophecies of Jeremiah, whose parallel language and repetition of what God taught "on the day that He took them out of Egypt" clarifies the meaning. In chapter 34 of the Prophet Jeremiah we read:

> Thus says the Lord of Hosts, the God of Israel, "I made a covenant with your fathers *the day that I brought them out of Egypt*, out of the land of slavery," saying: "At the end of seven years every man must free his brother who has been sold to him."
>
> Jeremiah 34:13–14

Obviously, Jeremiah is teaching that on the day immediately following the exodus there was one basic command which the Almighty wished to convey to His people: Do not enslave your brother, do not take undue advantage of your brother, do not manipulate your brother, do not make your brother a means for your personal end. Certainly this means that we may in no way harm our brother – and since the Almighty God created us all and is our sole parent in heaven, we are all brothers and sisters.

To be sure, there is room for offerings to God, for an expression of total commitment to the divine, for communal meals together with priests/teachers within the spiritual atmosphere of the holy Temple. Indeed, the Hebrew word *korban* (usually translated sacrifice) actually means "to come near." Apparently the sacrificial rituals are a means to an end, a way of attempting to approach the Almighty and to be able to sense His nearness; the sacrifices must be viewed within the context of "And they shall make for Me a Sanctuary so that I may dwell in their midst." The Sanctuary or the Temple, the sacrifices or the prayers, are all means to the ultimate end of walking with God and acting in accordance with His will. Unfortunately, there are times when the means can be substituted for the end, when the magnificent edifice becomes a substitute for God Himself, when rituals become so central that there is little room left for the acts of kindness they are supposed to inspire. After all, our human definition of God is a "Lord of love and compassion, kindness, patience and truth" (Ex. 34:6) – and having God in our midst means that we act in accordance with His divine characteristics!

Indeed, the Mishna recounts a horrible event which emphasizes the tragedy that can occur when the Temple ritual is not placed in proper context. Our rabbis have taught:

> The story is recorded that there were two priests racing up the ramp of the altar in a contest, the winner of which was to perform the Temple ritual of cleaning off the ashes (from the altar). When one seemed to be four cubits ahead of his friend, the other priest took a knife and pierced the heart of his opponent. Rabbi Tzadok stood on the Temple steps and said, "Our brothers of the house of Israel, listen well: If a corpse is found between two cities, the elders must bring a sacrifice; we must all make atonement." The father of the fatally injured priest found his son still in the last moments of his life. He cried out, "May this be your atonement; my son is still in the agony of the throes of death and so the knife has not been rendered impure." From this we see that the ritual purity of the vessels had assumed greater importance than a human life.
>
> *Yoma* 23a

Jeremiah bitterly mourned the destruction of the Temple and even cursed the day of his birth because he had to be the prophet of destruction. He understood the value of the sacrifices, but only if they were placed in proper context and were seen as a means to an end and not as an end in themselves. Indeed, because this was not the case, the Temple had to be destroyed. Hence the prophetic reading which is usually read after this portion of sacrifices, and which is read on the 9th of Av – the day of the destruction of our two Temples – concludes with the verse cited by Maimonides at the end of his *Guide for the Perplexed*, a message which all of Jewish tradition understands is the central focal point of our faith:

> Thus says the Lord: "Let a wise person not glory in his wisdom, let a strong person not glory in his strength, let a wealthy person not glory in his wealth. But only in this shall the one who glories glory: understand and know Me, because I am the Lord who does lovingkindness, justice and charity on earth. These are the things I want, says God."
>
> Jeremiah 9:22, 23

Shemini

Brides and Grooms, Feasts and Fasts

> *And it happened on the eighth day... of the*
> *consecration of the Sanctuary, which was the first*
> *day of the month of Nisan...*
>
> RASHI, LEVITICUS 9:1

The first day of the month of Nisan is a great occasion of joy within biblical history. It is the day when the Almighty declared His first commandment to Israel: "This renewal of the moon shall be to you the festival of the new moon; it is to be to you the first month of the months of the year" (Ex. 12:2). Indeed, the Midrash records that these divine words were heard throughout Egypt, because they foretold that a most significant event was about to take place on this first of the yearly months, the Israelite nation was about to be born as it leaves Egypt amidst great wonders and miracles, a stupendous change was about to transform the political and social character of the greatest power in the world, the Egyptian slave society (*hodesh, hidush,* month, change, novelty).

Therefore, the whole of the month of Nisan is considered to be a holiday, thus:

> We are not to fall on our faces (by reciting the penitential prayer
> *tahanun*) for the entire month of Nisan…, and we are not even
> to fast (during this month) for a *yahrzeit* (death anniversary of
> a departed parent).
>
> *Shulhan Arukh Orah Hayim* 429 with *Rema* gloss

The apparent reason for this festive quality of the month is the fact that
Nisan is the month of our redemption. And this is especially true for
Rosh Hodesh Nisan, the first day of the month of Nisan, when God's word
was heard throughout Egypt and the optimistic command of sanctifying the monthly renewal of the moon was given to Israel. Indeed, this
is probably the reason why the author of the Passover Haggada even
suggests that the *seder* ought to have taken place on *Rosh Hodesh* Nisan,
were it not for the requirement of matza and maror on the evening of
the 15th of Nisan.

And yet, the same Rabbi Moshe Isserles who forbids fasting on
a *yahrzeit* during the month of Nisan and who generally forbids a bride
and groom from fasting on their wedding day if they are married on any
Rosh Hodesh (first of the month) throughout the year – since a bride and
groom are forgiven all of their prior sins on their wedding day, they are
by custom enjoined to make the day before their wedding a mini Yom
Kippur fast up until the marriage ceremony – does specifically enjoin the
bride and groom to fast on *Rosh Hodesh* Nisan! (*Shulhan Arukh, Orah
Hayim* 572, Rema, Rabbi Moshe Isserles). Rabbi Yisrael Meir Kagan, the
Chafetz Chaim, agrees, although other authorities consider it "a great
wonder." How can we explain the tradition allowing a bride and groom
to fast on *Rosh Hodesh* Nisan?

The reason given by the Rema for the wedding fast is precisely
because of the horrific tragedy of which we read in the opening verses
of the biblical reading: The deaths of Nadav and Avihu, which occurred
specifically on the first day of the month of Nisan, the eighth day of
the consecration of the Sanctuary, the very day on which the Sanctuary was erected.

Why was a day of such religious sensitivity and significance transformed into such tragedy and terror? And why express the agony of what

was supposed to have been a day of ecstasy into the fast of a bride and groom on that day?

According to Rashi, Nadav and Avihu were righteous individuals, even more righteous than Moses and Aaron.

Why does the sanctification of the House of God require such sacrifices – the sincerely pious sons of Aaron, the High Priest? The sacred text doesn't explain itself, it merely ordains and decrees. The Divine Presence is a flame of fire – and fire purifies, purges, but it also consumes.

But why do we recognize the tragedy of the day – a day on which we still recite the usual Psalms of Praise (*Hallel*) of *Rosh Ḥodesh* – specifically by allowing the bride and groom to fast prior to their wedding ceremony if they are being married on that day?

The answer to this question is to be found in the Midrash which suggests that the commandment to build the Sanctuary was given only after the Almighty had forgiven Israel for the sin of the golden calf, on the morrow of Yom Kippur, the Day of Atonement. From this perspective, the Sanctuary became the nuptial home in which God and Israel were to dwell together forever, the supreme symbol that Israel had indeed been forgiven; from this moment onward, the major metaphor for the God-Israel relationship became that of bride and groom.

Hence every bride and groom are a reflection of God the groom and Israel the bride with the bond of matrimony reflecting a little bit of divine love and forgiveness. And just as every marriage has moments of tragedy as well as joy, of fasting as well as feasting, even God's subsequent relationship with Israel contained the zenith of our holy Temples and the nadir of our exiles. Ultimately, however, we know that God will redeem us, so that a Jewish marriage is an expression of faith in a glorious Jewish future despite our rootedness in blood, and of Jewish belief "that there will be heard in the streets of Judea and the great places of Jerusalem the sound of joy and happiness, the sound of bride and groom" despite our exile and persecution.

The death of Nadav and Avihu on the very day of the completion and final consecration of the Sanctuary was an expression of our realization that our marriage with God will be rocky as well as rapturous, will have moments of loving communication as well as moments of inexplicable isolation and abandonment. The young bride and groom similarly reflect the heartthrobs and heartaches of married life by their fast on *Rosh Ḥodesh*, as well as their faith in each other that they will overcome every challenge and emerge from their trials strengthened and redeemed. And so Aaron is silent, *"Vayidom Aharon,"* (Lev. 10:3) when faced with the tragedy of his sons' demise. He realizes that there are divine decrees which must be accepted even when they cannot be understood.

In a Munich Synagogue several years ago, I witnessed another kind of silence. There were about one hundred people in shul – but only the cantor and I were praying. Everyone else was talking – not in the hushed tones in which neighbors generally speak during the prayer service but in loud conversations, even occasionally walking from place to place as they spoke, seemingly totally unaware of the praying and Torah reading going on at "center stage." My host explained it very well: "These Jews are all Holocaust survivors or children of Holocaust survivors. They're angry at God – so they can't, or won't speak to Him. But neither can they live without Him. So they come to shul, and they don't speak to Him. But they do speak to each other…"

I believe that bride and groom must also learn from the congregation in Munich. There are often difficult moments in life, so difficult that you can't even speak to God, you can only be silent before the divine decree. But at these moments you must speak to each other, give to and garner strength from each other, attempt to find comfort in the miracle of your love for each other.

When Extra Becomes Excessive: Nadav and Avihu As Sinners

> *And Nadav and Avihu, the sons of Aaron, each took his censer, placed fire on it, and laid incense thereon, and offered strange fire which He had not commanded them. And there came forth fire from before God, and it devoured them, so that they died before God.*
>
> LEVITICUS 10:1–2

The portion of *Shemini* begins with the great drama of the week-long consecration ceremony of the Sanctuary. The nation is exalted, the leadership is inspired – but suddenly joy is turned into tragedy when the two sons of Aaron the High Priest are consumed by a fire sent down by God. What caused such a hapless event? The biblical text seems to say that it was because "they offered a strange fire which [God] had not commanded." What possible sin could these two "princes" in Israel have committed to make them worthy of such punishment?

What was this strange fire? The phrase is so ambiguous that the various commentaries offer a number of possibilities. Immediately after the deaths of Aaron's sons, the Torah issues a command forbidding Aaron and his sons to ever carry out their Sanctuary duties under the influence of any intoxicants. If a person cannot "…distinguish between the holy and the mundane, and between the unclean and the clean…" (Lev. 10:10) he doesn't belong in the *Ohel Moed* (Tent of Meeting). Thus it's not surprising that one midrash (*Vayikra Raba* 12:1) looks upon this injunction as a biblical hint that Nadav and Avihu were inebriated when they brought the incense offering, the intoxicant turning their incense offering into a "strange fire."

Another midrash explains that Nadav and Avihu so envied Aaron and Moses, that they couldn't wait for them to step down so that they could step up. This is the strange fire of jealousy which hadn't been commanded of them; they themselves initiated a sacrifice without asking permission of their elders, Moses and Aaron. They were too ambitious for their own good.

Rashbam writes that Nadav and Avihu were told not to bring the incense offering lest their fire diminish the glory of God's name and the miracle of the heavenly fire; nevertheless, they brought it and therefore were punished.

Rabbi Joseph B. Soloveitchik, my late rebbe and mentor, has often taught that in order to grasp how the sages wanted us to understand a given Torah portion, we should always turn to the *haftara* (the portion from the Prophets) for that week, which often serves as a commentary in and of itself.

Three separate events take place in the *haftara* of this portion, chapters six and seven in II Samuel. Thirty-thousand of the nation's chosen join with King David on his journey to restore the previously conquered holy ark to Jerusalem, turning the occasion into a celebratory procession accompanied with all kinds of musical instruments. The ark is transported in an oxcart that belongs to the brothers, Uzzah and Ahio; when the oxen stumble, Uzzah reaches out to take hold of the ark. Right then and there, God strikes Uzzah dead.

Three months pass before David again attempts to bring back the ark, and when he arrives triumphant in the city of Zion, he dances with all of his might, upsetting his wife who chastises him: "How did the king of Israel get his honor today, who uncovered himself today in the eyes of the handmaids of his servants, as one of the vain fellows who shamelessly uncovers himself" (II Samuel 6:21). The third incident records that David decides he wants to build a permanent dwelling for the ark of God rather than allowing it to rest in a curtained enclosure. At first the prophet Nathan is encouraging, but later in the night a voice tells him that although David's throne will be established to last forever, he personally will not build the Temple; his son Solomon will. In the account of the same event recorded elsewhere, the blood that David caused to flow in the various wars he fought prevents him from building a Temple which must be dedicated to peace (I Chronicles 22:8).

All three incidents point to the same theme: the emotional instinct of the individual has to take a backseat to the objective commandment of God, especially in the realm of ritual.

Uzzah certainly did not intend disrespect when he took hold of the ark; nevertheless, touching the holiest object in existence was forbidden. Since Michal is the daughter of King Saul, and knows first-hand that a king's honor is not his own but is rather the nation's, she cannot applaud David's leaping and dancing in wild abandon – even if it be in religious ecstasy. As such, the monarch of Israel must never lose his objective reason and allow emotion to dominate his behavior.

And as to who will build the Temple itself, King David himself must be ruled out because of all the spilled blood; his wars may have been necessary but even the most just of wars brings in its wake excessive killing, even killing of the innocent, emotional hatred and passionate zeal. What the *haftara* reflects back on is that performing a *mitzva* which God didn't command – no matter how inspired, spiritually or ecstatically – invites a disapproving, destructive blaze from heaven. Like Uzzah, Aaron's sons got too close to the sacred, took the sacred into their own hands. They went beyond God's command and beyond reason. The Torah avoids telling us the specific motivation behind the "strange fire" in order to underscore that it doesn't matter how laudable the purpose may be – if God didn't command it, it's forbidden. Ecstasy, even in the service of God, can become a disservice, turning the offering on its head; instead of expanding spirituality, it invites destruction.

It can often lead to righteous zealotry, to passionate pursuit of God's honor at the expense of human life and respect for others. Indeed, it is forbidden to serve God when intoxicated, when inebriated with one's passion rather than with one's reason; religious fire can turn into "self-righteous fanaticism" which can tragically lead to the desecration of the divine name, to suicide bombers.

There is yet another less dramatic lesson to be learned from Nadav and Avihu. Too much zeal in ritual can sometimes stop us from seeing the forest for the trees. We get so involved in a small detail – important as it may be – that it overwhelms the meaning of what our real goals ought to be. Nadav and Avihu added to the ritual demanded by God – but more is not necessarily better!

Adam warned Eve not to eat of the fruit nor to touch the tree, the second admonition having been his own. The midrash teaches that the snake pushed Eve against the tree, demonstrating that she could touch the tree without being hurt, and in one instant the serpent's battle of convincing her to eat the fruit was won. Adding to ritual can sometimes have the opposite effect; our sages teach us that by adding we sometimes subtract and detract.

Nadav and Avihu are rare Jews, sons of Aaron, nephews of Moses, their lives dedicated to service in the Temple, privileged to be among the chosen few to have had a sapphire vision of God's glory back at the sealing of the covenant in the portion of *Mishpatim*. We cannot even begin to comprehend their spiritual heights. Nevertheless, they die tragically. For one brief moment in their lives, they did not ask themselves if God commanded this extra fire or not. When people on the level of Nadav and Avihu fail to distinguish between divine will and human will, allowing their subjective understanding to take over, the punishment is instantaneous death. The rest of us may not call down a divine fire each time we substitute our own will for the will of God; nonetheless, we should realize that confusing the two is playing with fire. Excess in the ritual realm can often lead to zealotry and hypocrisy. It is enough to do what God commands. We can then be fairly certain that we are serving God and not our own ego, that we are acting in pursuit of divine Service and not excessive subjective passion. One dare not get too close to the divine fire, lest one get burnt by that very fire.

A Contemporary Postscript

The offering of Nadav and Avihu is biblically described as a "strange fire," *eish zara*, reminiscent of the Hebrew *avoda zara*, strange service, the usual phrase for idolatry. The Bible does isolate and emphasize a unique prohibition of fire idolatry, immolating one's child to the idol Moloch, a strange and false god who demands the fire consumption of children as the manner of his devotion. At least three times, the Bible specifically forbids this form of idolatry, "a strange service." Initially it is to be found in the biblical portion of sexual immorality, the prohibition of giving one's seed to a strange and uncertified place (someone else's wife, one's close relatives, individuals of the same sex, animals); within this context, the Bible commands, "And you shall not give of your seed (children) to be passed over to Moloch" (Lev. 18:21).

Barely one chapter later, the prohibition is fleshed out:

> An individual who gives his seed to Moloch must be put to death... And I shall put My face against that individual and cut him off from the midst of his nation because he has given his seed to Moloch, in order to defile My Sanctuary and profane My holy name....
>
> Leviticus 20:2

A third description of this abomination appears in the last of the five Books of Moses, "Let there not be found among you one who passes over his son or daughter into fire" (Deut. 18:10). Combining the various elements involved in the three verses similarity in language – "passing over one's child in fire to Moloch" – causes the Talmud to rule that the prohibition is literally sacrificing one's child in fire to the false god (*Sanhedrin* 64, Ramban on Lev. 18:21). Apparently, such an abominable act could only be performed in a moment of religious fanatic ecstasy, a moment in which one's false religious value took precedence over the life of one's innocent child. The "strange fire" brought by Nadav and Avihu was certainly not the same; but since it too emanated from a moment of religious ecstasy, such ill-advised and uncommanded fires had to be "nipped in the bud"!

Tragically, Islamic fundamentalism has adopted precisely this abomination as a major form of its terrorist activity: educating and training their youths to blow themselves up in the fire of destructive materials in the name of Allah and with the promise of a paradise of seventy-two virgins. Indeed, these "priests" are worse than the priests of Moloch: these modern-day human sacrifices are "inspired" not only to sacrifice themselves, but also to blow up scores of innocent people – children and women as well as civilian men – along with themselves!

The fourteenth-century scholar Rabbi Menahem Meiri taught that idolatry has little to do with thought – theology – and has everything to do with action – morality: an idolater is one who is "immorally defiled in his deeds and ugly in his personality traits" (Bet Habehira to Mishna 1 of *Avoda Zara* 2). Islamic fundamentalism has turned Allah into Moloch-Satan, and made every mosque which preaches the doctrine of suicide bombing a hell-haven of idolatry.

The Difficult Lesson of Divine Distance: a Time to Be Near, a Time to Be Far

> And Nadav and Avihu, the sons of Aaron, each
> took his censer, placed fire on it, and laid incense
> thereon, and offered strange fire which He had not
> commanded them. And there came forth fire from
> before God, and it devoured them, so that they
> died before God.
>
> LEVITICUS 10:1–2

The textual ambivalence regarding Nadav and Avihu reflects the complexity – and even tension – built into the very nature of the religious experience. Love of God engenders the desire to constantly feel the presence of the divine, to strive to become ever closer to the omniscient and compassionate Creator; fear of God engenders an awesome inadequacy, a sense of human frailty and transience, before the *mysterium tremendum* of the omnipotent and eternal ruler of the universe. Love of God inspires the individual to overcome all barriers, to push aside all veils, in a human attempt to achieve divine fellowship; fear of God fortifies the fences separating us from the Almighty, inspires us to humbly serve the author of life and death from a distance – without getting burnt by the divine fire.

From this perspective, herein lies the primary distinction between the priest and the prophet (the *kohen* and the *navi*). The priest is first and foremost the guardian of traditional laws and customs, ceremonies and prayers, which express the way in which we serve our God; these rituals are precisely defined to their every detail, have been time-honored and century-sanctified to provide historical continuity, a participation in the eternity of a rhythmic cycle which was there before I was born and will be retained after I die. Hence the priest receives his mandate from his father – from generation to generation – and wears special and precise clothing symbolizing the external form of divine service. These rituals provide structure, but rarely allow for spontaneity; they ensure continuity but leave little room for creativity. Undoubtedly, the sacred rite passed down from generation to generation serves as our bridge to eternity, a gateway to the divine; but it also erects a certain barrier, weaves a curtain of white parchment and black letters between the individual heart and mind and the Almighty God.

The prophet, however, wears no unique clothing and need not be born into a specific family. He attempts to push aside any curtain, break through whatever barriers in order to scale the heights and achieve divine nearness. He feels God's fire as "a fire which burns within his bones." He is often impatient with the details of ritual, the means which often cause him to lose sight of the ends; for him, passion takes precedence over protocol, spontaneity over structure.

The Jewish religious experience insists on maintaining the sensitive dialectic between love and fear of the divine, between the prophetic and priestly personality in divine service, despite and maybe even because of the necessary tension between them. You must cling to the Lord your God (*dvekut*); but do not draw too near to the mountain of the divine revelation lest you die. Allow for religious creativity and relevance by seeking the wisdom of the judge of each generation, but retain precedent by "asking your parent and he will tell you, your grandparent and he will say to you."

The Oral Tradition understands the necessity of sometimes abrogating a traditional law when a specific necessity warrants it – "It is the time to do for God, nullify your Torah" (Ps. 119:126) – but such extreme action is rarely invoked, generally giving way to obedience and humility in divine service. Prophet without priest threatens continuity and can even lead to frenzied fanaticism; priest without prophet can produce ritual without relevance, form without fire. Love God – but don't lose your sense of awe and reverence; rejoice in God, but not without a measure of trembling; strive to get close to the divine dwelling, but do not break through the door.

Nadav and Avihu were caught up in the religious ecstasy of the moment – and wanted to get even closer to God. Their motives may well have been suffused with divine love – but strange fires can lead to alien fanaticism, passion can breed perversion. They brought a strange fire – and God could not accept it. With all the inherent grief and tragedy, this was a time when the divine lesson had to be taught to all generations: sometimes "by those who are nearest to Me must I be sanctified" (Lev. 10:3).

The Message of Silence: Nadav and Avihu as Sacred Martyrs

And a fire came forth from before the Lord and consumed them; they died before the Lord.

LEVITICUS 10:2

The sudden deaths of Nadav and Avihu are a national tragedy for the nation of Israel, having occurred on the very day of the climax of the exodus from Egypt, at the very moment of highest tribute to the High Priest Aaron, symbol of divine protection and generational continuity. How ironic it is that Aaron's very future – the future of our nation, two young heirs to national leadership – is burnt in what appears to be a gratuitous and merciless act on the part of God.

The theological construct, expressed by Rashi, of somehow accepting as a fact of Jewish existence the sacrifice of our best and brightest, harks back to the haunting biblical scene at the very dawn of our history of the "covenant between the pieces." At its introduction comes the divine guarantee, "I am the Lord who took you out of Ur

Kasdim to give you this land as an inheritance" (Gen. 15:7). However, what immediately follows is the blood, smoke and fire of sacrifice, the prophecy that Jewish redemption requires a prelude – price of alienation, servitude and affliction on the part of the nation, and the understandable great, dark fear which descends upon Abraham as a result of his awesome vision. To be sure, the Covenant concludes in a confirmation of our continuity and territorial integrity; but our salvation will only come at the price of ultimate sacrifice:

> "And so the sun set, and a heavy cloud overcast. And behold, a smoking furnace of ashes and a torch of fire which passed between these [bloodied] pieces. On that day the Lord established His covenant with Abram, saying, 'To your seed have I given this land from the River Nile of Egypt to the Great River, the Euphrates.'"
> Genesis 15:7–8

From this perspective we understand the intermingling of the sacrificial blood of the paschal sacrifice with the joyous freedom of the wine which together mark our celebration of Passover – the "Hillel sandwich" which causes us to eat the matza of redemption together with the bitter herbs of suffering. And from this perspective, we understand why Yom HaZikaron, Israel's Memorial Day for her fallen martyrs of the IDF, enters into – and merges with – Yom Ha'Atzmaut, Israeli Independence Day, and why we are continually losing our most dedicated and committed people by terrorist attacks which comprise our present continuation of our War of Independence. And, amazing as it is, parents, spouses and orphans almost uniformly respond to these ultimate sacrifices as did Aaron of old, with a heavy, poignant and accepting silence.

As a very young boy, I remember attending the very first Shabbat circumcision ceremony celebrated by the Kloizenberg-Tzanz Hasidim after they located for a brief time in Bedford Stuyvesant, to where the community's remnants emigrated from the Holocaust before they were to settle in Netanya. The Rebbe, of blessed memory, recited the circumcision blessings, and with tears coursing down his cheeks could barely be heard as he choked upon the words, "And I see you rooted in your blood; and I declare unto you, by your blood shall you live, by your blood shall you live."

And then the rebbe spoke. He said the Hebrew word *damayikh*, "by your blood" can also be translated "by your silence" (*dom* is attentive silence, while *dam* is blood). We continue to live as Jews and propagate, and plant and build because – despite our tragic sacrifices – we remain silent before God, as did our forbear Aaron.

"However," he continued, looking upward and speaking with a voice which seemed to shake the very foundations of the building, "You, God, dare not remain silent." As the sweet Psalmist King David declared,

> Lord, You must not be silent (*al domi lakh*), You must not hush your voice, God, you must not be quiet, because, behold, Your enemies are shouting out loud...
>
> Psalms 83:2, 3

When Does Wine Bring Sanctity, and When Does Wine Bring Debauchery?

> *And fire came out from before the Lord and consumed [the two sons of Aaron] and they died before the Lord.*
>
> LEVITICUS 10:2

The Midrash provides the following explanation for the death of Nadav and Avihu:

> It seems impossible to understand why God would have caused them to die. And then comes the explanation in the verse which appears immediately after this incident; "And the Lord spoke to Aaron saying, do not drink wine or mead, neither you nor your sons with you, when you enter into the Tent of Meeting so that you do not die. It is an eternal statute for your generations so that you may distinguish between the holy and the profane, between the impure and the pure." *Vayikra Raba* 12:1

Apparently the Midrash is teaching that Nadav and Avihu were given this capital punishment because they had brought a fire unto God which had not been commanded while intoxicated with wine. From this perspective, wine – which removes the ability of the individual to distinguish between the holy and the profane, between the pure and the impure – can lead to evil action and can bring about tragic consequences. And indeed, according to the view brought down in the Talmud in the name of Rabbi Meir:

> The fruit from which Adam ate in the Garden of Eden was the fruit of the vine because there is nothing which brings greater woe to the individual than wine.
>
> *Sanhedrin* 70a-b

And of course it was Noah's planting of the vineyards which caused him to become drunk; the midrash even goes so far as to suggest that Satan was Noah's partner and convinced him to plant a vineyard and drink from its fruit.

At the same time, however, we have just concluded the festival of Passover whose first *seder* night is punctuated by four cups of wine which symbolize redemption. The Talmud goes on to teach, "There is no joy without wine since 'wine gladdens the heart of humanity'" (*Pesaḥim* 109a), and further enjoins that we "Remember [the Sabbath day] on wine" both at the inception of the Sabbath day, by means of the Kiddush, and at the closing of the Sabbath day, by means of Havdala. Is it not strange that the very wine which has the capability of causing forgetfulness, debauchery and drunkenness can also be used as a means toward sanctifying, understanding and distinguishing. After all, the very reference to Havdala (separation between the holy and the profane) is placed in the blessing in which we ask God to provide us with understanding and the ability to distinguish. In the words of our sages, "If there is no knowledge, how is it possible to distinguish between night and day, the Sabbath and the rest of the week, the holy and the profane?" And the blessing of Havdala is specifically recited over wine!

The Talmud links wine with the Hebrew word *tirosh*, which is usually translated as grape; *tirosh* is a rather complex noun, containing both the nuance of the Hebrew *rosh*, which means head, and the Hebrew *rash*, which means poverty. It is as if we are being warned that if the individual who drinks the wine has merit, he will become a head; if not, he will become a pauper. Wine, therefore, can lead the individual in two very opposite and even antithetical directions. It depends on the nature of the individual drinking the wine.

Maimonides, who first mandates that the joy of the festival must be expressed through meat and wine, goes on to distinguish between drunken frivolity and joyous festivity: "Drunkenness and much frivolity and levity is not rejoicing but is foolish hooliganism." We were not commanded to be foolish hooligans but rather to be joyous servants in the service of the Creator of all things. The Bible even states that "curses will come upon us because 'you did not serve the Lord your God in joyousness and good heartedness.'"

And later on, at the end of his "Laws of the Lulav "(8:15), "The joy with which the individual must rejoice is by means of doing the commandments and loving the Lord; such joy is a great act of divine service," an *avoda*, arduous and painstaking commitment, as in our preparations for Passover and Sukkot.

Rabbi Joseph B. Soloveitchik magnificently explains that the more energy the human being expends, the greater will be the sanctity and the deeper will be the joy. Ordinary juice is extracted from the fruit merely by squeezing it; wine is produced by the vine only by a long and an arduous process. It is for this reason that ordinary juice has an indistinguishable blessing (*shehakol*, which we recite over water), whereas wine demands a separate and unique blessing *borei pri hagefen* (Creator of the fruit of the vine).

Apparently Nadav and Avihu, at least according to the midrash we cited previously, went into the Tent of Meeting of the Sanctuary while intoxicated. The Sabbath wine, on the other hand, is a very different experience. We are commanded to "make" (*la'asot*) the Sabbath, and when we hold aloft the wine goblet of Kiddush, it is only after we have spent most of Friday (and often most of the previous week) in preparation for the holy Sabbath day. Wine which is drunk before one has expended energy and accomplished an ideal will lead to drunkenness; only wine which comes to express an inner state of sanctity and accomplishment as a result of successful human effort will lead to great joy. In the words of one of my great teachers, Rabbi Poleyoff: "If you are empty inside and expect the wine to put in the joy, the wine will only lead to forgetfulness and drunkenness; but if you are filled inside with a deep sense of self-worth and accomplishment – and you see the wine as an expression of your own state of human happiness – then the wine will lead to true rejoicing, sanctity and remembrance of the divine."

A Time to Speak, a Time to be Silent

> *Then Moses said to Aaron, 'This is that which the Lord spoke, saying, 'by those nearest to me must I be sanctified and in the face of the entire nation shall I be glorified. And Aaron was silent.*
>
> LEVITICUS 10:3

I n our previous commentaries on the portion of *Shemini*, we attempted to analyze the possible sin of Nadav and Avihu as a means of attempting to understand their tragic deaths. But there is another school of interpretation which views the incident very differently.

Rashi, the great commentator who faithfully conveys the most traditionally accepted rabbinical interpretations, views Aaron's sons as having been righteous and pure. He interprets Moses' words to his elder brother, "It is as the Lord has said, saying 'by my close ones shall I be sanctified and in the face of the entire nation shall I be glorified" (Lev. 10:3), as words of comfort:

Where did He [God] say 'By My close ones I shall be sanctified'? Do not read the verse "And I shall be sanctified by means
of My glory" (Ex. 29:43), rather read it to mean "by means of
My glorified ones"; Moses [therefore] said to Aaron, "Aaron, my
brother, I knew that this House would be sanctified by the most
beloved ones of God, and I thought it would be either through
me or through you. Now I see that they [Nadav and Avihu] were
greater than both of us."

Rashi, ad loc

Especially in light of this perspective, Aaron's response – or lack thereof,
as the Bible records, "And Aaron was silent, *vayidom Aharon*" – is to be
marveled at and pondered over. After all, Moses was the silent brother
described as "heavy of speech" and Aaron was the verbal, accepted
spokesperson; moreover, our tradition emphasizes the centrality of
speech communication not only as the major characteristic of humanity
(see Targum on Genesis 2:7) but also as a means of expressing – rather
than "locking in" – emotion, even if it is only to say at a time of tragedy, "Praised be the true Judge." How can we best understand Aaron's
biblically recorded silence at this defining moment in our early history?

I believe that the direction toward understanding may be derived
from a strange formulation of a midrash in the *Ethics of the Fathers*:

Rabbi Akiva says: "Tradition is a safeguard for Torah, tithes are
a safeguard for wealth, oaths are a safeguard for modesty, a fence
for wisdom is silence."

Avot 3:17

Generally, Rabbi Akiva expresses the safeguard, or fence, before the
value he is trying to protect; in the case of silence, the safeguard comes
last. Why the change in formulation?

I would suggest that in general it is speech, honest communication between people and especially academic lectures of Torah teaching,
which are the best protection and insurance for proper human relations,
study and wisdom; however, there are always unusual situations "of last
resort" when silence is the necessary "weapon of the last resort," when,

if the individual is forced to speak, he/she will only destroy a very special relationship. Then, at such times, it is silence which becomes the only – and final, last-ditch – option of wisdom.

The sages of the Talmud declare that the world is preserved only because of those who stop themselves from speaking out in difficult moments of strife (*Ḥullin* 89a), and even attribute to the Almighty the characteristic of silence in the face of those who desecrate His name. Perhaps the most acute example of a most painful but necessary silence is to be found "between the words" of a personal tragedy faced by our forefather Jacob.

Jacob has fought his battles with Esau, survived the challenge of exile and assimilation at the hands of his uncle Laban, overcome his grief at the loss of his beloved wife Rachel, and has finally returned home to the land of Canaan: "And it was when Israel dwelt in that land. Reuven went and lay with Bilhah his father's mistress and Israel heard." What then follows in all of the masoretic biblical parchments is an empty space, followed by a single brief biblical statement: "And the children of Israel were twelve" (Gen. 35:22). There is no recorded comment from the mouth of Jacob; apparently he remained silent.

I believe the Torah is "silently" portraying the complexity of reaction with which every wise parent can certainly identify. No matter what the true nature of Reuven's transgression with Bilhah might have been – according to rabbinic tradition, he switched his father's bed from Bilhah's tent to Leah's tent after the death of Rachel – he certainly acted in a manner hardly befitting any son, and certainly not the son of Jacob. The Patriarch must have been incensed, enraged – but at the same time, slightly guilt-ridden. After all, had he not also deceived *his* father, Isaac? And does Jacob himself not have a share in Reuven's transgression? Could we not possibly interpret Reuven's action as a cry for his rightful place as first-born, as his father's biological heir, a position which Jacob had denied him in favor of Joseph? Will not the Bible itself teach that a father dare not favor the younger son of the beloved wife over the elder son of the hated wife (Deut. 21:15–17)? And finally, for Jacob to speak out would be to have to banish Reuven from the family of Israel – and this Jacob was loath to do. A parent can never really become divorced from a child; the parent only hurts himself with such an act. Hence, the difficult but wisest course was to swallow his anger and his words, pursue a policy of silence, and thereby retain his relationship with his weak but suffering son. Hence, an empty space in the parchment scroll with the laconic but profound postscript to Jacob's silence: "And the children of Israel were twelve."

In one of the most powerful elegies in our liturgy, the *Eileh Ezkerah* description of the martyrdom of ten Talmudic greats during the Hadrianic persecutions which we recite on Yom Kippur, the angels in heaven cry out, "Is this the Torah and is this its reward?" The Almighty responds: "*Silence.* One more sound, and I shall turn the world back into water."

I was once present at a circumcision ceremony of a baby whose mother and grandparents were still mourning (sitting *shiva*) for the father, who had just been killed in the Yom Kippur War. He had been the only son of two people who were the sole survivors of their respective families after the Holocaust. I had paid a condolence call the day before – and the bereaved parents could not utter a word. They sat in silence, with tears occasionally falling from their eyes.

I was invited to name the baby, Yitzhak Abba ben Yitzhak Abba. As I intoned the blessing, which includes a verse from the prophet Ezekiel "And I see you rooted in your blood, and I say to you, by your blood shall you live, by your blood shall you live," almost everyone wept and wailed – almost everyone, since the bereaved parents remained silent.

I remembered what I had learned as a child, that *damayikh* can mean your blood – "by your blood shall you live" – and *damayikh* can also mean silence, *vayidom Aharon* – "by your silence shall you live." There are moments when it is possible to go on only if one remains silent, only if one is wise enough to understand that only silence, as difficult as silence may be – will not test and strain a relationship which has become fragile enough through tragedy but which is, in the final analysis, more precious than life itself. This is our legacy derived from Aaron's silence.

You Are What You Eat

> *Speak to the children of Israel, saying: Of all the*
> *animals in the world, these are the ones that you*
> *may eat. Among mammals, you may eat one that*
> *has hooves that are cloven, and that brings up its*
> *cud.*
>
> LEVITICUS 11:2–3

Jews are unique for many reasons, but one of our most unique aspects is our laws of kashrut. Kosher, both the word and the concept, has certainly penetrated the English language; not only is it a description of certain rigorous rules relating to food, but its use now applies it to areas of legitimacy. "Is it kosher?" a gentile real-estate magnate might well ask his assistant who has just presented his boss with an outline for putting together a certain real-estate deal.

Shemini introduces us to the laws of kashrut.

… of all the animals in the world, these are the ones that you may eat. Among mammals, you may eat one that has hooves that are cloven, and that brings up its cud.

Leviticus 11:2–3

The text further insists that only fish with fins and scales may be consumed. And we have very specific laws of slaughtering – which, in the main, stress as quick and painless a death as possible for the animal – as well as a process of salting and soaking the meat in order to get rid of as much of the blood as possible ("for the blood is the life-soul" [Lev. 17:14]); and finally there is the prohibition of eating meat and milk together ("Thou shalt not seethe a kid in its mother's milk" [Ex. 23:19]).

In addition to the message of moral ambiguity involved in consuming meat – and the concomitant issue of compassion for all creatures which limits our meat intake – what and where a Jew will eat goes a long way in determining Jewish identity. From a sociological perspective, one of the most important ways Jews kept together as one ethnic community despite our close to two thousand-year-long exile in lands all over the globe was due to our insistence on the laws of kashrut. It may truly be said that even more than the Jews kept kosher, the laws of kashrut kept and preserved the Jews from assimilation. One of the interesting things about the portion of *Shemini*, where we are first given the laws of kashrut, is that this portion always follows the festival of Passover (except during leap years, when a thirteen-month year causes a readjustment of all the weekly portions). I would like to suggest that the appearance of *Shemini* after Passover is most significant, on the basis of an idea suggested by the Pri Tzadik, in his Torah commentary.

It has been said that Jews may be characterized as a people who love to eat and speak; just witness a Jewish organizational dinner or attend a Jewish wedding or *bar/bat mitzva* and you can see the truth of this description. But it is interesting to note that the festival of Passover – and specifically the night of the *seder* – commands these two exercises by divine mandate: "And you shall *tell* your children" of the Egyptian servitude and exodus; "And in the evening you shall eat matzot." The *seder* is truly the mother of all Jewish dinners.

Indeed, it is only on the evening of Passover that we recite a blessing on the act of eating itself: "Blessed art thou O Lord our God, Ruler of the world, Who made us holy by His commandments and commanded us to observe the *eating of matza*." Matza, as a form of wheat, receives its due blessing as bread, whose formulation we know is "who brings forth bread from the earth." At the *seder*, and only at the *seder*, all of Israel make blessings which sanctify the specific act of eating, *"al akhilat."*

According to the Pri Tzadik, who emerges from the Kabbalistic and Hassidic traditions, this particular stress on eating, a blessing over the eating of matza and over the eating of maror, and, in Temple times, over the eating of the paschal lamb, is a repair or fixing (*tikkun*) for Adam and Eve in the Garden of Eden, whose cardinal sin involved eating a forbidden fruit from the tree of knowledge of good and evil.

In what way was Adam the human being different from the other animals in God's creation? First, Adam and Eve were the only creatures in Eden with the ability to verbally communicate (Targum to Genesis 2:7), and only Adam, in contradistinction to the animals and beasts, was given a commandment, and this commandment related to the act of eating:

> "And the Lord God commanded the human being saying: 'Of all the fruits of the garden you may surely eat, but of the tree of knowledge of good and evil you may not eat....'"
>
> Genesis 2:16, 17

Food represents all physical pleasures; it even serves as metaphor for sexual enjoyment (Gen 39:6). The Almighty, by His solitary commandment to Adam, is defining the human being as one who is to enjoy the physical aspects of this world ("from all the fruits you may surely eat"), but at the same time must discipline him/herself by limiting his/her consumption; in this way the human being becomes endowed with sanctity, and is given the challenge of sanctifying every aspect of the physical world around him. Man and woman may glory in their physical natures as well as in the manifold magnificent aspects of physical nature surrounding them; but they must at the same time uplift, ennoble and sanctify themselves and their world.

Tragically, Adam and Eve failed this, their first test and their solitary command. Humanity's exile and alienation from God, mankind's original slavery, in effect begins when Adam and Eve are driven out of the Garden of Eden. As punishment, from that point onward acquiring food would no longer be a simple matter. "Thorns also and thistles shall it [the earth] bring forth, and you shall eat of the herb of the field. By the sweat of your face shall you eat bread…" (Gen. 3:18–19). Food would become the focus of life – but it would be the acquisition and preparation of food, and it would require great effort and hardship.

When Israel emerges as a nation, the first festival they celebrate is the holiday of Passover. The *seder* is indeed the mother of all dinners – because it celebrates and sanctifies special foods as a means to an end, as an aspect of lovingkindness by sharing with those who are hungry, a symbol of transforming ancient memory into personal family experience, as an important but preparatory element in a drama established to communicate the importance of human freedom and praise to God. It is an act of eating which is truly a *mitzva*, a repair for the primordial act of forbidden eating which brought death to humanity.

From this perspective, we can readily understand how the laws of kashrut in the portion of *Shemini* continue the lesson of the Passover *seder* in teaching us how to sanctify the physical world through our attitude toward food.

Kashrut is our way of saying "no" to the serpent forever waiting in the wings.

And kashrut still remains a challenge to observant Jews in the modern world. Ought we not take the spirit of the law at least as seriously as the letter of the law by including in our kashrut inspection hygienic cleanliness, fair competition, and proper payment to and treatment of workers? Since the hoisting and shackling of animals are in no way a necessary aspect of proper ritual slaughtering – but do seem to add to the discomfort of the animal – how can we countenance such a procedure in our slaughter-houses? How can we sign on statements of kashrut certification for goose and veal – and serve these foods in our most "fervently observant" establishments – when we know the pain caused to these animals by force-feeding? And how can we continue to provide kashrut certification for places that sell cigarettes?

* * *

Family Postscript

Many decades ago, my eldest daughter – who was then four or five – was invited to a birthday party of a friend who did not come from a kosher home. I offered to supply the birthday cake – but it had already been purchased (from a non-kosher bakery). I gave Batya a choice: not to go to the party, to attend the party but not to eat, or to bring along her own chocolate cupcake. After thinking for a few minutes, she decided on the last option. She then said: "Abba, I'm really very lucky. My friend Bina is allergic to anything which is chocolate. I'm only allergic to anything which is not kosher."

Tazria-Metzora

God, What Have You Done for Me Lately?

> If a woman has conceived seed and born a male
> child: then she shall be unclean for seven days; as
> in the days of her menstrual sickness shall she be
> unclean.
>
> LEVITICUS 12:2

One of the greatest miracles of life is that of childbirth – and this Torah portion opens with the short state of impurity (bound up with the women's and child's close brush with death) and the much longer state of purity (because of the marvelous phenomenon of the continuity of life) which the mother must experience. And the Bible also commands the mother to bring two sacrifices (obviously during Temple times): a whole burnt offering, symbolizing the fact that all of life ultimately belongs to God, and a sin offering, usually explained as being necessary in case the woman took an oath never to become pregnant again while experiencing the pain of childbirth. What is strange about all this is that the mother is *not* commanded to give a thanksgiving offering, the most likely sacrifice one would expect to find in such a situation!

There is yet a second question – specific to the thanksgiving offering. The general law regarding a thanksgiving offering is that it must be completely consumed on the day on which it is brought – one day and one night. The priests eat of it their allotted portion, those who bring it eat of it, and others in Jerusalem may be invited to eat of it – as long as it is consumed by the end of the first night. Since many wealthy people would bring especially generous thanksgiving offerings in accordance with their station in life, and since the meat had to be consumed in one day, Josephus records that there was always plenty of "barbecued" meat offered to residents of and pilgrims to Jerusalem in open "Kiddushes" free to everyone. This certainly added an extra incentive to travel to Jerusalem for the pilgrim festivals – good food, free of charge, was always in abundance! But the thanksgiving offering is merely one type of sacrifice subsumed under the more general category of peace offerings (*shlamim*) – and all of the other peace offerings, like those brought in payment of an oath, may be consumed for two days! Why only give the thanksgiving offering one day to be eaten?

I would like to suggest an answer to both questions, but we must first review the fascinating biblical account of Elijah the Prophet on Mount Carmel. You will remember that Elijah, sorely vexed by the multitude of Israelites following the pagan god Baal, arranged for a daring contest in front of six hundred thousand Israelites, involving four hundred and fifty prophets of Baal versus the lone Elijah – on top of Mount Carmel. The prophets of each arranged their respective altars, the Baalists prayed, danced, sang and slashed their skin to their idol – but received neither answer nor response. Elijah turned heavenward:

> Answer me O God, answer me..., and a fire from the Lord descended and consumed the whole burnt offering...The entire nation saw, fell on their faces and said, "The Lord He is God, the Lord He is God"... and they slaughtered the false prophets of Baal.'
> 1 Kings 18:37–40

The story, however, is not yet over. Ironically and tragically accurate is the response of Jezebel, wicked and idolatrous Queen of Israel, to Elijah: "At this time *tomorrow* I shall make your life like each of those [slaughtered prophets]" (ibid. 19:2). Why the next day, and not that very day? After all, the powerful and diabolical Queen Jezebel could just as easily have ordered an immediate execution for Elijah! But she understood that had she done so on the day of the miraculous occurrence, when Elijah was a national hero, she may well have faced a popular uprising. Tomorrow, however, one day later – by then, the miracle would have been forgotten, business would return to usual, and the wicked queen could do whatever she wanted to Elijah with impunity. Her words ring so true that Elijah flees to the desert and begs the Almighty to take his soul!

The Bible, as well as our own contemporary experiences, abound with supportive incidents to buttress Jezebel's insight. Only three days after the miracle of the splitting of the Reed Sea, the freed slaves again complain about the bitter waters at Mara. Only forty days after the phenomenal revelation at Sinai, the Israelites worship the golden calf – and the day after the miraculous Six Day War and the liberation of Jerusalem, the Jews in the Diaspora as well as in Israel largely returned "to business as usual." Indeed, Moshe Dayan, when he first visited the Western Wall, kissed its stones with such visible emotion that a reporter asked if he had become a "born-again Jew." Dayan honestly responded, "I was not religious yesterday and I will not be religious tomorrow. But at this moment, no one in Israel is more religious than I."

This is how Rabbi Naftali Zvi Yehuda Berlin, famed nineteenth-century dean of the Volozhin Yeshiva, answered our questions. It is sadly not within the nature of most people to sustain our feelings of thanksgiving; we are generally only concerned with what God has done for us *lately*, now, today. We all too easily forget God's many bounties of yesterday – and certainly of last year and of five years ago. The offering for thanksgiving must therefore be consumed on the very day it was brought; by the next day, the feelings of gratitude will have dissipated. And since the woman may not offer a Temple sacrifice after childbirth until the periods of her impurity and purity have passed – forty days for a male child and eighty days for a female child – she cannot be expected to bring a thanksgiving offering such a long time after the birth. By then she may be so concerned with staying up at night and the vexations of a colicky offspring that the initial joy of birth may well have been forgotten.

Love, Marriage and Continuity

> *If a woman has conceived seed and born a male child, then she shall be unclean for seven days; as in the days of her menstrual sickness shall she be unclean. On the eighth day [the child's] foreskin shall be circumcised. For thirty-three additional days, she shall sit on blood of purity....*
>
> LEVITICUS 12:2–4

The Torah reading of *Tazria* is not only difficult because of its subject matter – the ritual status of a woman after she gives birth in terms of the times when she is ritually impure and when she is ritually pure, as well as the ritual impurity which devolves upon both men and women when semen or blood emerges from their bodies – but also in terms of the very strange order of the verses and the chapters.

The first question arises from a verse which seemingly has no connection with what precedes or follows it: after the Bible has informed us that when a woman bears a male child she will be ritually impure for seven days (Lev. 12:1, 2), the following verse does not deal with the subsequent thirty-three days of ritual purity which she is allowed to enjoy no matter what her physical state may be – that comes two verses later (Lev. 12:4) – but rather the Bible informs us "That on the eighth day the flesh of his foreskin shall be circumcised" (Lev. 12:3). Why have the law of circumcision in the very midst of the laws of a woman's status of purity upon her giving birth? It hardly seems to belong!

The second question deals with the order of the chapters. Chapter twelve deals with ritual purity and impurity as a result of childbirth, as we have seen. Chapter fifteen deals with the different kinds of seminal emissions which emerge from a male and the different kinds of blood emissions which emerge from a female; emissions which are also connected to reproduction as a result of a sexual act between the couple. In the midst of these two biblical discussions, which certainly involve ritual impurity and impurity surrounding reproduction, come two chapters – chapters thirteen and fourteen – which deal with *tzara'at*, usually translated as leprosy but which certainly refers to a discoloration and degeneration of the skin, which causes the individual to look like a walking corpse. Why bring *tzara'at* in the midst of a discussion on reproduction?

In Rabbi Joseph B. Soloveitchik's important work entitled *Family Redeemed*, my revered teacher interprets the opening chapters of Genesis as a crucial lesson to humanity concerning the spiritual potential as well as the destructive danger of the sexual act. Indeed, the classical commentator Rashi understands the fruit of knowledge of good and evil as having injected within human nature libido, eroticism and lust, rather than the expression of love and the reproductive powers which were initially embedded in human nature. Sigmund Freud sees the serpent as a phallic symbol and "eating" is often found in the Bible as a metaphor for engaging in sex. From this perspective, the sin of having partaken of the forbidden fruit is the sin of sexual lust, which can often separate sex from the sacred institution of matrimony, a natural expression of affection between two individuals who are committed to a shared life and to the establishment of a family.

It is fascinating that the punishments for having eaten the fruit are related to reproduction:

> "And to the woman He said, 'I will greatly multiply your pain and travail in pregnancy and with pain shall you bring forth children....'"
>
> Genesis 3:16

Even more to the point, the most fundamental penalty for having tasted of the forbidden fruit is death, which plagues men and woman alike: "But of the tree of knowledge of good and evil, you shall not eat; for on the day that you eat of it you shall surely die" (Gen. 2:17). The sexual act was meant to give not only unity and joy to the couple but also to bestow continued life through the gift of reproduction. Tragically the misuse of sex and its disengagement from love, marriage and family can lead to death inducing diseases such as AIDS.

I would argue that this is precisely why *tzara'at*, or the living death which it symbolizes, appears in the Bible in the midst of its discussion of reproduction and the normative processes of seminal emissions and menstrual blood, which are necessary by-products of the glory of reproduction. Tragically the life-force which is granted by God through the sexual organs can often degenerate into decay and death when those very sexual organs are misused.

I will also submit that this is precisely why the commandment of circumcision comes right before the biblical establishment of a large number of days of purity (thirty-three after the birth of a male and sixty-six after the birth of a female), no matter what blood may emerge from the woman's body. The much larger number of days of purity attest to the great miracle of childbirth – which is always a heartbeat away from death for every anxious parent until the healthy baby emerges and emits its first cry (and this accounts for the initial days of ritual impurity), but which results in new life and the continuation of the family line, giving the greatest degree of satisfaction that a human being can ever experience. Such glories of reproduction are only possible if the male will learn to limit his sexual activity to within the institution of marriage and will recognize the sanctity of sex as well as its pleasures. Placing the divine mark upon the male sexual organ with the performance of the commandment of circumcision establishes this ideal of sanctity. The sacredness of the woman's body is similarly expressed when she immerses herself in a *mikveh* prior to resuming sexual relations with her husband each month and even makes a blessing to God while still unclothed within the ritual waters, which symbolize life and birth and future.

Hence, the most meaningful blessing which I know is intoned during the marriage ceremony: "Blessed are You O Lord our God, King of the Universe, who sanctifies his nation Israel by means of the nuptial canopy and the sanctity of marriage."

Humans Must Perfect Themselves

> *And on the eighth day the flesh of his foreskin*
> *shall be circumcised.*
>
> LEVITICUS 12:3

As mentioned in the previous chapter, the commandment of circumcision in the portion of *Tazria* appears right in the middle of the discussion of the impure and pure periods immediately following childbirth. Furthermore, our sages specifically derive from this ordinance that the ritual of circumcision overrides the Sabbath:

> On the eighth day, [the child's] foreskin shall be circumcised –
> even if it falls on the Sabbath.
>
> *Shabbat* 132a

Why express this crucial significance of circumcision – it takes precedence even over the Sabbath – within the context of ritual impurity? Is there a connection?

Targum Yonatan Ben Uziel links the two issues by interpreting:

And on the eighth day, when [she] is permitted [to have sexual relations with her husband], on that [day] is [the baby] to be circumcised.

He is thereby citing the view of our sages in the Talmud, who understand that the circumcision must be on the eighth day following the birth "so that everyone not be happy while the parents will be sad" if they cannot properly express their affection toward one another (*Nidda* 31b).

It seems to me that there is a more profound connection. When a woman is in a state of ritual impurity, she and her husband are forbidden from engaging in sexual relations until she immerses in a *mikveh* (ritual pool of rain or spring water). Obviously this restriction demands a great deal of self-control and inner discipline. The major symbol which graphically expresses the importance of mastering one's physical instincts is the command of circumcision: even the sexual organ itself, the physical manifestation of the male potency and the unbridled id, must be tempered and sanctified by the stamp of the divine.

A well-known midrash takes this even one step farther:

> Turnus Rufus the Wicked once asked Rabbi Akiva: "Whose works are better, the works of God or the works of human beings?" He answered him, "The works of human beings…" [Turnus Rufus] said to him, "why do you circumcise?" [Rabbi Akiva] said, "I knew you were asking about that, and therefore I anticipated [the question] and told you that the works of human beings are better." Turnus Rufus said to him: "But if God wants men to be circumcised, why does He not see to it that male babies are born already circumcised?" Rabbi Akiva said to him…"It is because the Holy One Blessed be He only gave the commandments to Israel so that we may be purified through them."
>
> *Midrash Tanḥuma, Tazria, 5*

Rabbi Yitzhak Arama, in his commentary *Akedat Yitzhak*, explains this to mean that there are no specific advantages or necessary rationalizations for doing the commandments; they are merely the will of God, and we must see that as being more than sufficient for justifying our performance of them.

It seems to me, however, that the words of the midrash as well as the context of the commandment reveal a very different message. The human being is part of the physical creation of the world, a world which is subject to scientific rules of health and illness, life and death. The most obvious and tragic expression of our physicality is that, in line with all creatures of the universe, we humans as well are doomed to be born, disintegrate and die. And therefore the most radical example of ritual impurity is a human corpse, *avi avot hatuma*. However, an animal carcass, a dead reptile, and the blood of the menstrual cycle (fall-out of the failed potential of fertilization) likewise cause ritual impurity. A woman in childbirth has a very close brush with death – both in terms of her own mortality as well as during the painful anguished period preceding the moment when she hears the cry of a healthy, living baby.

God's gift to the human being created in the divine image, however, is that in addition to physicality there is also spirituality, in addition to death there is also life eternal, in addition to ritual impurity (*tuma*) there is also ritual purity (*tahara*). Hence, the very human life which emerges from the mother's womb brings in its wake not only the brush with death, *tuma*, but also the hope of new life *tahara* – and while the *tuma* is for seven days, the *tahara* is for thirty-three! The human being has the power to overcome his physical impediments and imperfections, to ennoble and sanctify his animal drives and instincts, to perfect human nature and redeem an imperfect world.

This was the message which Rabbi Akiva attempted to convey to Turnus Rufus the Wicked. Yes, the world created by the Almighty is beautiful and magnificent, but it is also imperfect and incomplete. God has given the task of completion and redemption to the human being, who has the ability and capacity to circumcise himself, to sublimate his "sub-*gartelian*" (beneath the *gartel*, or belt) drives, to sanctify society and to complete the cosmos. Indeed, the works of the human being are greater! And the command of circumcision belongs within the context of impurity and purity.

And this is also what our sages were trying to convey when they taught that circumcision overrides the Sabbath. The Sabbath testifies to God's creation of the world – impressive but imperfect, awesome but awful, terrific but tragic. Circumcision testifies to the human being's challenge to redeem himself and perfect the world. Indeed, circumcision overrides the Sabbath.

The Miracle of Childbirth: A Brush with Death

And when the days of her purifying are fulfilled for
a son or a daughter, she shall bring a lamb of the
first year for a burnt offering and a young pigeon,
or turtle dove, for a sin offering, to the door of the
Tent of Meeting, to the priest, who shall offer it
before God and she shall be cleansed...

LEVITICUS 12:6–7

Not surprisingly, the occasion of childbirth is so momentous that the Torah commands sacrifices to be brought after the birth.
What does surprise many people is that the Torah ascribes ritual impurity – *tuma* – to a woman after childbirth – and distinguishes between
the birth of a boy and the birth of a girl as to the number of *tuma* days.

If it's a boy, the mother brings the sacrifice after waiting forty days,
the first seven days in a state of impurity (*tuma*) followed by thirty-three
days of purity (*tahara*). And if it's a girl, the waiting period for bringing

the sacrifice is eighty days, this time counting fourteen days of impurity and sixty-six days of purity.

Why does the Torah stress the sex of the child in determining the mother's state of ritual being. Is there any scientific or experential difference in the process of giving birth which might account for this ritual difference based on the child's gender?

There is however, an even more fundamental question to be asked. Regardless as to whether the period is seven days for a boy and fourteen days for a girl, why should the woman be *tamei*, ritually impure, at all? What is *tuma*, biblical ritual impurity, all about? How and why does it come into existence?

If one were to search for a conceptual scheme, I believe that the ascriptions of ritual impurity in the Bible are all related to the movement away from life and toward death. Unlike the Egyptian *Book of the Dead*, our Bible is a book of Life! We are biblically exhorted "to choose life" and God views the totality of his living creation as good (Gen. 1). Anything which militates against life and expresses death is declared *tamei*, ritually impure; hence the severest form of such impurity is a human corpse, which is called the grandfather of all ritual impurities (*avi avot hatuma*). Animal carcasses and reptile remains are likewise ritually impure, as is the leprous individual whose limbs are wasting away and who gives the specter of living death.

Not only death itself, but even the unfulfilled potential for life also creates *tuma*. This is the source for the *tuma* of a menstruating woman. Every month, the ovum produced in a woman's body is ready for fertilization and the birth of new life. But if this process doesn't take place, the blood vessels that would have nurtured the fetus burst, resulting in the monthly flow of blood. The sight of blood means that the potential for new life was not fulfilled, that the new life which was prepared for arrival would not make the scene. Hence, a pregnant woman does not menstruate: Her blood cells are nurturing the new life growing inside the womb. From this perspective it is easy to understand why the antidote, or cure, for ritual impurity is an immersion in a *mikveh*, a pool (or well-spring) of running water. Water is the symbol for life itself; the *mikveh* waters are even biblically called "living waters" (*mayim hayim*), and all of life emerged from water at the time of creation: "And the spirit of

God hovered over the face of the waters" (Gen. 1:2). The very word for *mikveh* comes from the Hebrew root for gathering as well as for hope: where there is life, there is hope.

Our question is now intensified! Why does the Bible speak of *tuma* altogether in the context of childbirth? The creation of new life ought to result exclusively in *tahara*, purity, with no reference to *tuma* at all?

The truth is that childbirth is that exquisite and awesome moment when death and life come together. I would like to suggest that the mother's impurity comes from the fact that every woman who gives birth has a serious brush with death. During labor, suffering may become so intense that the mother actually believes she is about to die. If something does go medically wrong, any doctor will testify that all of nature converges to save the child even at the expense of the mother, and, until only seventy-five years ago, the greatest cause of death among women was childbirth. In fact, a woman who gives birth is required to recite *birkat hagomel* (the blessing of thanksgiving) in the presence of a quorum in the synagogue, the same blessing said after every successful encounter with death. The blood in the wake of childbirth is reminiscent of the element of death present in that mysterious moment which hovers between life and death.

Since childbirth was only a brush with death, because mother and child do emerge intact, the days of purity far outweigh the days of impurity, in a ratio of either seven to thirty-three, or fourteen to sixty-six. And everything is doubled in the case of the birth of a girl, because it is the female physiology in which the death-life drama is played out.

This juxtaposition between death and life is not at all strange. The two come together at every serious operation; the "binding of Isaac" proves that only one who is willing to sacrifice his life for a higher ideal actually lives a meaningful life. In Israel we experience such a death-life connection with Yom Hazikaron, the Memorial Day for the soldiers who fell in Israel's battles for existence, coming the very day before Yom Ha'atzmaut, Israel Independence Day.

Emerging from the encounter with death of Yom Hazikaron, Yom Ha'atzmaut expresses the fact that the painful birth and continuing existence of Israel is a result of the tragic sacrifices of its soldiers.

The contiguous placement of Yom Hazikaron (brush with death and destruction, and Yom Ha'atzmaut; (the birth of the State of Israel) parallels the Torah's understanding of childbirth. *Tazria* does not only deal with the birth of a child; it leaves us with an existential understanding of the inextricable relationship not only between life and death, but also between purity and impurity. We come to learn that just as death and life are intimately, painfully and mysteriously connected, so too the states of purity and impurity exist in an eternal dialogue.

I cannot think of any moment in the year more poignant than the closing moments of Yom Hazikaron, as thousands gather in the large square in Efrat in the waning light of the day, a lone plaintive *Kel Maleh Raḥamim* prayer piercing the sky, slowly giving way to the thunderous explosion of fireworks celebrating Yom Ha'atzmaut.

May our celebrations of life always be far more numerous than our memorials to the dead.

Walls Which Speak in Red and Green

> *The Lord spoke to Moses and to Aaron saying,*
> *"When you come into the Land of Canaan which I*
> *give to you as an inheritance and I shall give you*
> *the plague of leprosy in the houses of the land of*
> *your inheritance."*
>
> LEVITICUS 14:34

The disease known as leprosy has engendered dread in the hearts of people, especially in times gone by when it was apparently more widespread and exceedingly contagious. In biblical times, the priests (*kohanim*) would determine whether a skin discoloration or scab was indeed leprous – and, if so, the hapless leper would be rendered ritually impure and exiled from society. From the biblical religious perspective, this *tzara'at* emanated from a serious moral deficiency, generally identified as slander.

An especially problematic aspect of these laws of *tzara'at* is the fact that not only individuals but even walls of houses could become infected by this ritually impure discoloration. Do walls have minds, souls, consciences or moral choices which allow for punishment? And stranger still, the Bible describes the phenomenon of "leprosy of houses" in almost positive, gift-of-God terms:

> "The Lord spoke to Moses and to Aaron saying, "when you come into the Land of Canaan which I *give* to you as an inheritance and I shall *give* you the plague of leprosy in the houses of the land of your inheritance."
>
> Leviticus 14:34

How are we to understand this biblical reference to the "divine gift" of the leprous walls? And third, for individuals, the *tzara'at* malady is expressed as a white discoloration, whereas for walls, white spots are not at all problematic, the only thing they attest to is mold! Green and red are the dangerous colors for walls (Lev. 14:36 ,37). Why the difference?

Nahmanides, the twelfth-century commentary who is an especial champion of the unique importance of the Land of Israel for the people of Israel, sees the phenomenon of the leprous walls as an expression of the intensely concentrated moral sensitivity of our holy land: the sanctity of Israel, home of the Divine Presence (*Shekhina*), cannot abide within its boundaries a home in which slander is spoken. Hence the walls of such a house in Israel will naturally show the effects of words of gossip which can destroy lives.

Maimonides sees another benefit to the "leprosy of the homes"– an explicit warning to cease and desist from speaking slander: "This is a sign and a wonder to warn people against indulging in malicious speech (*lashon hara*). If they do recount slanderous tales, the walls of their homes will change; and if the inhabitants maintain their wickedness, the garments upon them will change" (*Mishneh Torah*, Laws of the Impurity of *Tzara'at* 16:10).

Rashi suggests a practical application for the "gift of the leprous walls": "It was a happy tiding for them when the plague (of leprosy) came upon (their homes). This is because the Amorite Canaanites had hidden treasures of gold in the walls of their homes during the forty years when Israel was in the desert, and because of the leprous plagues the walls were taken apart and [the treasures] were found" (Rashi, Lev. 14:34).

I would suggest that Rashi's commentary may be given a figurative rather than a literal spin. The walls of a house represent a family, the family which inhabits that house; and every family has its own individual culture and climate, scents and sensitivities, tales and traditions. A house may also represent many generations of families who lived there; the values, faith commitments and lifestyles which animated those families and constituted their continuity. The sounds, smells and songs, the character, culture and commitments which are absorbed – and expressed – by the walls of a house, are indeed a treasure which is worthy of discovery and exploration. The walls of a home impart powerful lessons; hidden in those walls is a significant treasure-trove of memories and messages for the present and future generations. Perhaps it is for this reason that the nation of Israel is called the *house* of Israel throughout the Bible.

From this perspective we can now understand the biblical introduction to "house-leprosy." This hidden power of the walls is a present as well as a plague, a gift as well as a curse. Do the walls emit the fragrance of Shabbat *ḥalla* baking in the oven or the smells of cheap liquor? Are the sounds which seep through the crevices sounds of Torah study, prayer and words of affection or are they experiences of tale-bearing, porn and anger? The good news inherent in the leprosy of the walls is the potency of family: the very same home environment which can be so injurious can also be exceedingly beneficial. It all depends upon the "culture of the table" which the family creates and which the walls absorb – and sometimes emit.

With this understanding, it is instructive to note the specific colorations – or discolorations – which render the walls ritually unclean: "And he (the *kohen* – priest) shall examine the leprous plague penetratingly embedded in the walls of the house, whether they are bright green or bright red…" (Lev. 14:37). Can it be that green is identified with money and materialism (*yerukim* in modern Hebrew, an apt description of American dollars) and red identified with blood and violence? A home which imparts materialistic goals as the ideal and/or insensitivity to the shedding of blood – remember that our sages compared slander or character assassination to the shedding of blood – is certainly deserving of the badge of impurity! And is not the Palestinian flag waved so ardently by suicide bombers, red and green and white (white being the initial sign of leprosy).

And finally, Rashi suggested that there was an Amorite-Canaanite treasure which the inhabitants placed in the walls of their homes in Israel while the Israelites dallied in the desert rejecting the divine challenge of the conquest of Israel. Might not this interpretation be suggesting that the indigenous seven nations, as well as present-day Palestinians, do indeed have a treasure which they impart to the children through the walls of the houses? This treasure is the belief that the land is important, that the connection to the land is cardinal for every nation which claims a homeland and respects its past. The land must be important enough to fight and even die for, since it contains the seed of our eternity; only those committed to their past deserve to enjoy a blessed future.

I am certainly not suggesting terrorism against innocent citizens and nihilistic, Moloch-like suicide bombing, which perverts love of land into a rejection of life and destruction of fundamental humanistic values. The Torah declares the ritual impurity of Red, Green and White! But many Israeli post-Zionist leaders are forgetting the indelible linkage between a nation and its land as an expression of its commitment to eternal ideals and the continuity between its past and future. Tragically we all too often only begin to appreciate the importance of our homeland when the Palestinian suicide attackers threaten to take it away from us by their vicious attacks. But perhaps sacred lessons can even be learned from purveyors of impurity.

An Open Heart and a Closed Hand

> *And his servants came near, and spoke to him,*
> *and said, "My father, if the prophet had asked*
> *you to do some great thing, would you not have*
> *done it? How much rather then when he says to*
> *you, Wash and be clean?" Then he went down*
> *and dipped himself seven times in the Jordan,*
> *according to the saying of the man of God, and*
> *his flesh was restored like the flesh of a little child,*
> *and he was clean.*
>
> HAFTARA OF TAZRIA, II KINGS 5:13–14

The two Torah portions of *Tazria-Metzora* deal with a malady similar to what we know as leprosy – but it is apparent from the text (and especially from the interpretation of our sages) that the source of the disease is a spiritual rather than a physical imperfection. I believe that the two *haftara* portions – or, more correctly, the unread prophetic passage – provide a fascinating insight into what that spiritual imperfection might be. Moreover, both prophetic readings teach all subsequent generations what Israeli leadership requires in order for our nation to succeed.

The *haftara* for *Tazria* is taken from the second book of Kings; it deals with the miraculous way in which Elisha, prophet of the Lord, succeeded in curing the leprosy of Na'aman, powerful general of the armies of Aram. However, the incident surrounding Na'aman's cure is the subject of the fifth chapter; the *haftara* begins, strangely enough, with the concluding three verses of the previous chapter, which tell how Elisha is able to alleviate the hunger of one hundred people with a comparatively small amount of food. This odd introduction seems to have nothing to do with the subsequent story of Na'aman or the disease which links the incident in the book of Kings to this Torah reading.

As the story unfolds, we learn that Na'aman was "general of the armies of the King of Aram, a great man before his master…a courageous soldier and – a leper" (5:1). A captive Israeli maiden suggests to Na'aman's wife that her husband seek a cure from Elisha, the prophet man-of-God of Israel. After an initial request, "Elisha sends to him (Na'aman) a messenger, who says:

> Go and bathe [immerse yourself] seven times in the Jordan River; your flesh will then be restored and shall be purified.
>
> II Kings 4:11

After the words of the prophet are proven to be efficacious, a most grateful Na'aman exclaims: "Behold, now I know that there is no God anywhere in the world except in Israel; and now [Na'aman requests of Elisha] please accept a gift from your servant" (5:15). Elisha, the man of God, refuses, upon an oath to God, to accept anything; Na'aman is so moved by what has transpired that he asks for a small parcel of land in which he can build an altar and offer sacrifices to the one true God of Israel and the world. And so concludes the *haftara* for the Torah reading of *Tazria*.

The following *haftara* for *Metzora* continues with chapter seven of the second book of Kings (note that chapter six is deleted from the public prophetic readings), and opens with a tale of four lepers outside the gate of the city. There is apparently a bitter war going on between

Israel and Aram – as well as rampant hunger in Israel so acute that mothers are eating their own children. As a result of Elisha's intervention, the famine ends; the four lepers bear the happy tidings that the Aramean encampment has miraculously been evacuated, the Aramean Army has defected, and Israel has emerged victorious. This prophetic reading concludes by describing the death of the chief courtier of the King of Israel: he is trampled by the hordes of Israelites rushing to pillage the Aramean encampment. Apparently he was punished for having cynically questioned Elisha's prophecy concerning the end of the famine and the success of Israel.

A number of startling questions emerge as we read these *haftarot.* The first reading concluded with a grateful Aramean general convinced that the God of Israel is the only true God of the world. What has caused him, only one chapter later in the second book of Kings, to wage war against the very people who were responsible for the cure of his leprosy? And of what relevance to the subject of leprosy are the opening story of Elisha's feeding of the poor and the concluding story of the trampling to death of the Israel courtier?

I believe that we will discover the clue to our understanding by reading the end of the fifth as well as the sixth chapter of the second book of Kings (deleted from the public *haftara* readings, which include only the beginnings of chapters five and seven), and by taking note of Rashi's identification of the four lepers of good tidings as Gehazi and his three sons (Ibid 7:3).

Who was Gehazi? The second book of Kings records (in the passage not publicly read) that after Elisha refused to accept any gift from Na'aman for having effectuated his cure, Gehazi "the lad [go-fer] of Elisha man-of-God" ran after the Aramean general; claiming to have been sent by his master Elisha, he requests a *kikar* of silver and two changes of clothes for two prophets-in-training (Elisha's *kollel*, as it were). Na'aman readily complies, generously giving two kikars of silver in addition to the outfits of clothes. When Elisha discovers what his factotum has done, he punishes him: "The leprosy of Na'aman shall cling to you and to your children forever" (Kings II 5:27). The next thing we learn is that Israel is suffering a grievous famine and is under siege by the armies of Aram.

Apparently Na'aman – as well as God – had turned against Israel.

What caused the sudden disaffection? Clearly it was the greed of Gehazi for two kikars of silver. Elisha's storming sanctification of God's name had been turned into a devastating desecration of God's name! Na'aman had certainly been impressed with Elisha's ability to cure him – but he had known of similar acts bordering on sorcery which emanated from the pagan world. What had really impressed the general of the armies of Aram was that Elisha was a true man-of-God, an individual who did what he did purely for the sake of Heaven with no ulterior motive for personal gain. It was only at that point – when Elisha refused to take any compensation whatsoever – that Na'aman decided that he only desired to give sacrifices to the God of Israel.

But when Gehazi entered the scene with his greedy desire for some silver and clothing, Na'aman understandably became disillusioned. He now sees Elisha as just another sorcerer – and if so, he is even ready to wage another war against his former enemy.

The second message of these Prophetic Readings is the necessity of the people of Israel – and especially the leaders of Israel – to believe in the future of the covenantal nation, to have faith that Israel will ultimately be saved by God. The courtier of the king cynically questioned Israel's deliverance, and he therefore deserved to die.

Perhaps both of these messages are inextricably bound together. Only when we have completely selfless leaders – who give of themselves purely for the sake of Heaven and nation without the expectation of even a scintilla of personal gain – do we have the right to expect that God will intercede on their (and our) behalf. Such a leader was Elisha, prophetic man-of-God, in the opening verses of the *haftara* of *Tazria*. Elisha proves to be such a leader when he punishes Gehazi for his venal act of greed with the disease of leprosy – apparently a fitting punishment for the sin of inordinate materialistic desire. The courtier should have realized that when Israel is guided by selfless leaders who rise above the blandishments of bribery and material compensation, God will always enable His nation not only to survive but truly to prevail.

Aḥarei Mot

Be Passionately Moderate!

> And God spoke to Moses after the death of the
> two sons of Aaron, when they came near before
> the Lord and died.
>
> LEVITICUS 16:1

Which is the greater evil in God's eyes – hot sins of passion or cold sins of apathy? Rabbenu Zadok HaKohen of Lublin (1822–1900), in his masterful work *Pri Zaddik* on the portions of the week, cites a famous midrash of an individual walking on a road (life's journey), seductively being summoned either by fire to his right or snow to his left. The wise traveler understands that he must remain at the center, avoiding both extremes of either fanatic passion (fire) or disinterested apathy (snow). But which of the two extremes is more problematic?

A sin of apathy – symbolized by snow – could well describe the infamous transgression of the scouts, tribal chiefs sent by Moses to bring back a report about the land of Israel. Although they did not conceal the positive aspects of the Promised Land (flowing with milk and honey, and grapes so huge eight men were required to carry each cluster), ten of the scouts nonetheless stressed the negative: a race of people descended from giants who would be impossible to conquer. At the end of the day it was their (and the nation's) apathy toward Israel and disinterest in the religious and political challenge and potential of national sovereignty, which led them to take the path of least resistance and either return to Egypt or remain in the desert. Their sin was one of coldness and disillusionment, a lack of idealism bordering on cynicism.

In contrast to the apathy of the spies, the classic example of a sin of passion may be ascribed to Nadav and Avihu, Aaron's sons who died when they brought an unauthorized offering of "strange fire," referred to in the beginning of this Torah portion. The initial event describes the dedication of the Sanctuary, amidst all of the pomp and circumstance of the priestly ritual, which achieves a climax when the Almighty sends down a fire from heaven to consume the sacrifice of the Israelites and to demonstrate His acceptance of their service. The people become exultant, fall on their faces in worship! And in this moment of ecstasy Nadav and Avihu, sons of the high priest and major celebrants at this consecration, express their passion for God in bringing a "strange fire which had not been commanded." They are immediately killed by God in a fire from above. It seems clear that here is the prototypical "sin of fire," excessive ecstasy which – if not tempered by divine law – can lead to zealous fanaticism which must be stopped in its tracks.

Nevertheless, I would argue that in the scale of transgression, "sins of fire" are generally more forgivable than are "sins of snow." Even if Nadav and Avihu committed a transgression in bringing their strange fire, Moses mitigates their crime when he communicates God's reaction to his bereft brother:

> I will be sanctified through them that come near to me, and before all the people will I be glorified.
>
> Leviticus 10:3

The sense of the verse is that although the transgression had to be punished, the perpetrators of the crime are still referred to as being "near" to the divine. In contrast, the apathy of the spies leads to major tragedies throughout the course of Jewish history, starting with the punishment of the entire desert generation.

> They will therefore not see the land that I swore to their ancestors.
> Numbers 14:23

Moreover, the self-imposed passion of Nadav and Avihu, although it leads to the tragic deaths of these two ecstatic celebrants, does not go beyond the "transgressors themselves"; the Bible adds a further commandment several verses after the description of their death:

> Drink no wine or strong drink... when you go into into the Tent of Meeting, that you die not...
> Leviticus 10:9

In effect, the Bible is forbidding unbridled ecstasy within divine service. But this is a far cry from the punishment of the Ninth of Av tragedy (the day of the scouts' report) which portends Jewish exile and persecution for thousands of years!

Finally, one most striking feature of this portion's opening verse, which refers back to the trangression of Aaron's sons who "came near before the Lord and died," is the absence of the names of Nadav and Avihu. Could the Torah be distinguishing the act from the actors, the crime from its perpetrators? Passion that can lead to fanaticism must be stopped and condemned, but the individuals, whose motives were pure, remain close to the Almighty even in their moment of punishment! And despite the fact that excessive passion resulted in the deaths of Nadav and Avihu, the service in the Temple goes on. Once again, in contrast, when the ten tribal heads refuse to enter the land, they are in effect saying no to the entire plan of God; Jewish history comes to a forty-year standstill because of the apathy, and faithlessness of the scouts.

Rabbenu Zadok goes one step further in his interpretation, explaining the root cause of sins of apathy. Why do people or nations fall prey to the snow of icy coldness and disinterested paralysis? What gives rise to a cynical dismissal in place of an idealistic involvement? It is the individual's lack of belief in his capability to succeed in the activity;

cynical nay-saying can often serve as a protection against failure and disappointment. Remember how the scouts described the giant inhabitants of Canaan:

> We were in our own eyes as grasshoppers, and so we were in their eyes.
>
> Numbers 13:33

The majority of the scouts began with a poor self-image, and since they cannot possibly imagine defeating the Canaanites, they decide not even to attempt it.

This connection between cold apathy and low self-image is hinted at in a verse of the song of praise, *Eshet Hayil* – "Woman of Valor" (Proverbs 31:10–31) sung at the Friday evening Sabbath table. Most of the verses praise the initiative and lovingkindness of a woman "who considers a field and buys it" [31:15] and "stretches out her palm to the poor" (31:20). But how are we to understand the verse:

> She is not afraid of the snow for her household, for all her household are clothed with scarlet.
>
> Proverbs 31:21

Had the verse mentioned warm, woolen garments I would have understood the reference, but how does being clothed specifically in scarlet garments protect from snow? However, if we consider snow as a metaphor for sins of apathy, then the verse is telling us a simple truth: the woman of valor is not afraid that her household will suffer from apathy and disinterestedness, a paralysis of action such as that which afflicted the generation of the scouts, because she imbues in them deep feelings of self-worth; she dresses her household in the royal garb (scarlet). If you wish your children to emerge as kings, then bring them up like princes!

Now, if too much fire leads to death, then it might be better to choose snow over fire, and do away with the unique priestly garments which are liable to produce the exaggerated emotion of zeal! After the double deaths of Nadav and Avihu, one might speculate that if the voltage in the holy Temple is so high, the danger involved may not be worth the risk. With the death of his sons, it would have been natural for Aaron to question his capacity to serve as high priest. Maybe he even blamed himself for the deaths of his sons because of his involvement at the debacle of the golden calf – thinking that he had not done enough to dissuade the Israelites from succumbing to their idolatrous tendencies. At that time, most of the Israelites went wild and off-course with ecstatic abandon, and now his own sons went too far with their "Holy Temple" passion.

But apparently that is not the biblical perspective. After the reference to the deaths of Nadav and Avihu, this Torah portion continues with a description of the special garments Aaron must wear in order to officiate on the Day of Atonement.

> He must put on a sanctified white linen tunic, and have linen pants on his body. He must also gird himself with a linen sash, and bind his head with a linen turban. These are the sacred vestments.
>
> Leviticus 16:4

I would submit that here the Torah is emphasizing that we dare not throw out the baby with the bathwater. National and religious pride must still be nurtured and fostered despite the fiery fanaticism which can sometimes emerge from special unique garb and inspiring divine service. What we see from this discussion is that although both passion and apathy have inherent dangers, the results of apathy can be far more devastating in the long run.

However, in the final analysis, if we return to our midrash about the individual who must walk in the middle of the road, neither falling prey to the fire – to the successive passion – nor to the snow, to the apathetic loss of idealism, we realize that to remain in the center is not to take a path of least resistance; it is rather the Golden Mean of Maimonides, "the truest path of sweetness and road of peace" as demarcated by our holy Torah, whose "tree of life is in the center of the garden." The traveler must zealously guard against either extreme. Yes, the Hassidic Kotzker Rebbe taught: "Better a 'hot' *misnaged* (opponent of the Hassidic movement) than a 'pareve' *hassid*!" But best of all is one who is passionate in his moderation, and understands that either of the extremes can lead to disaster.

How Yom Kippur Works

> *For on this day He will forgive you, to purify you*
> *from all your sins; before the Lord you shall be*
> *purified.*
>
> LEVITICUS 16:30

The major source for the awesome, white fast known as Yom Kippur, or the Day of Atonement, is to be found in the Torah portion of *Aharei Mot*.

It is fascinating to note that while Yom Kippur is the most ascetic day of the Hebrew calendar, a twenty-five-hour period wherein eating, drinking, bathing, sexual relations, bodily anointment and leather shoes are all forbidden, it is nevertheless considered a joyous festival, even more joyous than the Sabbath (Yom Kippur nullifies the seven-day mourning period after the death of a close relative, whereas the Sabbath does not). The great Hassidic sage Rabbi Levi Yitzchak of Berditchev would often say, "Even had the Jewish tradition not commanded me to fast during our two major fast days, I would be too mournfully sad to eat on Tisha B'Av and I would be too excitedly joyous to eat on Yom Kippur."

From whence the excitement, and from whence the joy? It seems to me that Yom Kippur is our annual opportunity for a second chance, our possibility of becoming forgiven and purified before God. On the festival of Matzot we celebrate our birth as a nation; seven months later on the festival of Yom Kippur we celebrate our rebirth as human beings. On *Pesaḥ* we renew our homes and our dishes, routing out the leavening which symbolizes the excess materialism and physical appurtenances with which we generally surround ourselves; on the Day of Forgiveness we renew our deeds and our innermost personalities by means of repentance.

Despite the hard work entailed in pre-Pesaḥ cleaning, and in due deference to the hardy Jewish men and women who spend so much quality time tracking down all traces of leavening and thoroughly destroying them, such a physical cleaning job is still much easier than spiritual purification. Such a repentance is at least a two-step process, the first of which is *kappara* (usually translated as "forgiveness" and literally meaning "a covering over") and the second *tahara* (usually translated as "purification" and literally meaning "a cleansing.") These two divine gifts of the day correspond to the two stages or results of transgression. The first is a stain or an imperfection in the world as a result of an act of theft or the expression of hateful words. The second is a stain on the individual soul as a result of his/her committing a transgression. Rabbi Joseph B. Soloveitchik believed that *kappara* – paying back the theft, asking for forgiveness by saying I am sorry, or bringing a sacrifice to the holy Temple – removes the first stage. *Tahara* – the repentance of the soul, the decision of the individual to change his personality and to be different from what and who he was before – removes the second. *Kappara* is an act of *restitution*, utilizing objects or words; *tahara* is an act of *reconstitution* of self, which requires a complete psychological and spiritual recast.

Clearly *kappara,* restitution – paying the debt, bringing the offering, beating one's breast in confession – is much easier to achieve than a reconstitution of personality. How does Yom Kippur help one pass the second phase? How can an individual on a particular date acquire the requisite spiritual energy and profound spiritual inspiration to transform his/her inner being to be able to say: "I am now a different person; I am not the same one who committed those improper actions?"

I believe the answer is to be found in the manner in which we celebrate Yom Kippur. It is a day when we separate ourselves from our materialistic physical drives in order to free our spiritual selves to commune with God; the purpose of this separation is not to make us suffer but rather to enable us to enjoy the eternal life of the spirit in the presence of God.

We leave behind our homes and good clothes; our cars, wallets and credit cards; our business offices and cell phones; our physical drives for food and sex; and remain in the synagogue for a complete day, garbed in simple white dress and virtually naked before the loving Creator of the universe, who is ready to accept, forgive and purify us.

Indeed, Franz Rosenzweig, a Jewish theologian of the early twentieth century, entered university as a completely assimilated Jew. He decided to convert to Christianity, which he understood to be the advanced stage of Judaism. However, he decided that the most intellectually sound path for him to take was to graduate from Judaism *into* Christianity. He therefore began to study the biblical and Talmudic texts, and went to synagogue on Rosh Hashana and Yom Kippur. He told his friend Rosenstock-Huessy that the prayer experience on Yom Kippur was so intense that he knew by the conclusion of the day that he would remain a Jew all of his life and would devote whatever time God gave him to live to study the faith of his forebears.

If we truly internalize what the day of Yom Kippur is trying to say to us, it can become a truly transforming experience. It is this kind of inspiration that Yom Kippur hopes to effectuate as we stand in God's presence for a full day: "Before the Lord shall you be purified" (Lev. 16:30). And this is the message of Rabbi Akiva at the end of the Tractate *Yoma*:

> Fortunate are you Israel! Before Whom are you purified and who purifies you – our Father in Heaven…. The Lord is the *Mikveh* of Israel: just as a *mikveh* purifies those who are impure, so does the Holy One Blessed be He purify Israel.
>
> Mishna *Yoma* 8:9

This World or the Next World – Which is Paramount?

> *And you shall observe My statutes and My laws*
> *which people shall perform and shall live by them,*
> *I am the Lord.*
>
> LEVITICUS 18:5

Heaven and hell and the world to come are the bread and butter of most of the world's religions. In various shades and using different metaphors, the terrors of hell and the splendors of the kingdom of heaven are portrayed in living color: the Islamic paradise is the green of the gardens of Eden, and the Christian hell is black night and fiery red. The major focus of most religions – from as far back as the Greek mythological figure, Charon, who ferried the dead from this world to the next, and the Egyptian bible, which was called the *Book of the Dead*, to the more contemporary Christianity, which venerates the cross of crucifixion and celebrates the resurrection of the founder of Christianity – seems to be the world-to-come and the best way for each one to get there.

Judaism certainly accepts the idea of the world-to-come as a fundamental truth. Despite the absence of specific after-life references in the Torah, the introductory words to the *Ethics of Our Fathers*, probably the most popular of our *Mishnayot* and part of our Sabbath afternoon liturgy, declares that all of Israel has a share in the world-to-come. And although there may be no direct references to an after-life, there is an indisputable basis for the eternality of the soul in Genesis: "And God created the human in His image, in the image of God He created him, male and female he created them" (Gen. 1:27). The human created in the divine image is more than a complex animal; he/she possesses a soul, a spirit, a psyche, a spark of the divine. And just as the Almighty is eternal, so must the divine spark within the human being be eternal, and so must that spark endow every human being with the gift of eternity. Hence death is not final; the human soul lives eternally in another dimension of existence, in the world of the spirit. And although the Torah doesn't go into specifics on the number of rooms in heaven or how many angels can dance on the head of a pin, it's clear that the world-to-come is taken for granted. Indeed, we need to go no further than chapter five in Genesis to find the best way, the Torah way, of looking at death:

> And Enoch walked with God and he was not, for God took him.
> Genesis 5:2

The last stop for the human being is not the cemetery; it is rather the dimension to which God takes him, the world-to-come. Indeed, one of the most common expressions for death in the Bible is that the individual was "gathered to his people," was returned to join the souls of those loving family members who left this world for the other eternal dimension of life after life. This biblical phrase echoes the studies of Elizabeth Kubler Ross, who documents the experiences of many different patients from many different ethnic backgrounds who were declared clinically and medically dead, but were subsequently revived. They invariably tell of having felt an incredible peacefulness, of moving through a tunnel with a significant light emanating at the end of it, and having met close family and friends who had previously "died" and were now greeting them just beyond the dazzling light on the other side.

Nevertheless, it is fascinating that the Bible, unlike so many other traditions, not only does not record graphic descriptions of heaven and hell, but also does not even emphasize the importance of the world-to-come. One of the reasons why not may well be because a religion based on an after-life is generally predicated more on fear of death than on appreciation of life, fear of punishment rather than reverence for God. Moreover, the powerful and hypnotic spells that a description of other-worldly delights and castigations can bring casts over its adherents the kind of hysterical ecstasy which can lead to suicide bombers and will-ful immolations. But most important of all, a religion which focuses on the other world has a tendency to downplay this world; after all, if this world is only temporary and the other world is eternal, it is hardly worth the effort to even attempt to right the wings of injustice and to alleviate the suffering of poverty and pain!

An even greater insight into this biblical truth is emphasized by the verse quoted:

> And you shall observe My statutes and My laws which people shall perform and shall live by them, I am the Lord.
>
> Leviticus 18:5

This phrase "you shall live by them" has been made to assume a cardinal position by the sages of the Talmud (*Yoma* 85b): "you shall live by them," and not die by them: this is true even if it means violating a command as significant as the Sabbath in order to save the life of another human being!

Perhaps the reason why the Torah avoids all other worlds except ours is because it knows the dangers of exploiting the weaknesses, fears and fantasies of a beleaguered population by emphasizing for them the other worldly delights, causing them to forget present hardships and even court martyrdom. Our task is to make this world a better place – this land, this century, now – for the betterment of mankind.

In the opening law of his section on "Sanctifying God's Name" in his monumental work, *Mishneh Torah* – a section in which we would expect the great legalist to praise martyrdom – Maimonides opens his discussion by generally forbidding the Jew to give up his life for the sake of a Torah commandment; there are only three exceptions to this rule, which are idolatry, murder and sexual immorality (incest and adultery). In effect, says Maimonides, we sanctify God by living! The Torah, unlike the Egyptian *Book of the Dead*, is the Hebrew book of the Living. Life, not death, is the message of Judaism. Before we concern ourselves with paradise above, we have to create a paradise below. Jerusalem must become a city of righteousness, a city which teaches ethical monotheism and world peace in order for it to be considered a city of God. Many people erroneously think that the best way to sanctify the name of God (*Kiddush Hashem*) is through martyrdom, but the real sanctification emerges from how we bring holiness into this mundane, insane and sometimes ugly world. Maimonides describes and defines the highest fulfillment of sanctifying God's name when a Torah scholar:

> Speaks softly and kindly to all creatures, respects even those who denigrate him and comports his business dealings in good faith....
> *Mishneh Torah*, Laws of Yesodei Hatorah 5:10

One of the key moments in Jewish history is Abraham's near-sacrifice of his son Isaac when he obeys God's command to bring his beloved child as a "whole burnt offering." But despite all the existential anguish of the meaning of the divine request, the bottom line is that Abraham is then told "not to cast a hand upon the lad, not to do him any harm." God concludes this nightmarish episode with the resounding message that He doesn't wish Isaac to die for Him, but rather to live in dedication to His laws. And the sages of the Midrash refer to Isaac as the "unblemished whole burnt offering, *olah temima, after* he descends from the mountain, living a life dedicated to the just and compassionate laws of God.

The central image of Christianity is the martyred death of its founder crucified on the cross; in contrast, the central image of Judaism is the six-cornered shield of David, who fought in order to live and rule, or the Sanctuary's menora which symbolizes the Tree of Life in the Garden of Eden. Our goal is not so much to reach the other world, but is rather to transform this world into the peaceful and harmonious Garden of Eden.

When Rabbi Israel Salanter, the nineteenth-century founder of the Mussar movement, was confronted with a raging cholera epidemic one Yom Kippur, he knew that a decree to break the fast and eat in order to strengthen oneself would be met with disapproval. In David Frishman's short story, "Three Who Ate," based on a historical account of this episode, the author describes how during the night of *Kol Nidrei*, the sexton read the names of everyone who had died during the course of that terrible summer. The next morning, after the reading of the Torah, Rabbi Salanter announced that everyone must make Kiddush lest their fast make them susceptible to the disease. A murmur went through the congregation. Yom Kippur?! No one moved. Again the rabbi commanded the worshippers to make Kiddush. Silence!

To the astonishment of the assembled, the rabbi asked for cake and wine, and called over two judges. In the presence of the entire congregation he made Kiddush, adding the blessing, "…who commanded us to live by them, my laws."

What makes Judaism different? Although our history has brought us again and again to the valley of death, we revel in and constantly celebrate our survival and our mission to repair and rectify this imperfect world.

"To live by them" means just that: to live. Thus it's obvious why we are so driven and concerned with the survival of the Jewish State. In the end it's not the heavenly Jerusalem toward which we direct our passions, but the Jerusalem down below, the one with hills, pink-veined stones, and vibrant light. It is Jerusalem, the City of Return, to which we have come after two thousand years of exile; it is Jerusalem, the City of Life, which symbolizes our renaissance and rebirth; it is Jerusalem, the City of Peace, which expresses our aspirations for this world's redemption. Jerusalem was the place where Abraham took Isaac to near death and witnessed his return to life. Jerusalem is the place from where the Messiah will invigorate the entire world with the joy of re-creation.

Whose Life Is It Anyway?

> And you shall observe My statutes and My laws
> which people shall perform and shall live by them,
> I am the Lord.
>
> LEVITICUS 18:5

A recent Broadway show was entitled "Whose Life Is It Anyway?" Conventional wisdom would certainly have it that our lives belong to us and that we have ultimate authority over what we do or do not do with and to our bodies. Judaism, however, may very well have a very different perspective.

We read in this Torah portion, "And you shall observe My statutes and My laws which people shall perform and shall live by them, I am the Lord" (Lev. 18:5). As we have seen earlier, our sages extract from the words "and shall live by them" that we must use Torah as a means to a more sanctified life rather than a reason for martyrdom.

However, the verse we've just cited, which seems to be a resounding declaration for life over law, serves as the introduction to a long list of forbidden sexual relationships – and acts of sexual immorality, along with idolatry and murder, are the "exception to the rule" cited above; they are transgressions over which we are commanded to surrender our lives rather than commit. If that's the case, why does the command that we live by our laws introduce specifically those laws for which we must be willing to die?

I would argue that the real interpretation of the verse "You shall observe My statutes...and live by them" is that an individual who is truly God-fearing must be willing to live in accordance with God's law and not in accordance with his own desires or decisions. It is God's laws which must become the prescription for our lives; it is God who tells us how to deal with our bodies and when we may or may not sacrifice our lives. In a very real sense, Judaism would insist that from a theological perspective, our lives belong not to us but to God, because after all it is God who is the author of life, who gives us our lives and our bodies and therefore insists on defining what we may or may not do with them.

This is perhaps one of the critical differences between the mentality of Western culture and our own Jewish traditions. From the perspective of Western culture, sexual activities are completely outside the province of ethics and morality. Two consenting adults can do anything they wish with their bodies and with each other's body; even married partners who agree to the kind of open marriage that permits sexual promiscuity would not at all be frowned upon by liberal defenders of individual autonomy. The biblical command which insists that we live by God's laws and statutes tells us that our bodies belong to God and our sexual mores must be expressed in accordance with God's will. It is God's body, not ours!

It is from this perspective that suicide is prohibited by biblical law (Rashi on Gen. 9:5) since life – although our sages recognize how incredibly difficult life can sometimes be – is nevertheless seen as a divine gift which no individual can decide at will to snuff out. As is well known, the issue of human autonomy versus divine rights is one of the basic issues of medical ethics today. Liberal America insists that every mother has the intrinsic right to abort a child because the fetus is part of her body and no one can tell her what she can or cannot do with her own physical being. Similarly, if, for religious reasons, a particular individual refuses to accept a blood transfusion or a necessary operation, it is his inalienable right to make this decision. The only question that is presently before the courts is whether an individual has the right to make such a decision for his sick child. In other words, one's self and one's body includes one's fetus which is lodged in one's body; whether or not it also includes a born child who was already separated from its mother's body is a moot question which must be decided by the judiciary.

Jewish tradition has a very different take. And if Jewish law does not automatically forbid abortion (since the Mishna in *Ohalot* rules that "ensoulment" occurs at birth rather than at conception), it certainly disallows abortion as simply another means of birth control; for Jewish law, the fetus remains potential life, which requires a substantial mitigating factor such as danger to the mother or severe genetic damage before a fetus may be aborted. The biblical command that our control over our bodies and very lives is circumscribed and decided by the parameters of Jewish law, and the special permission granted doctors to heal (Ex. 21:19), point to the fact that if medical opinion demands that a leg be amputated in order for the patient to live, the patient does not have the right to refuse the operation. Recently, there was a woman in Israel who refused to have her gangrenous leg removed because she argued that the future world is the eternal world and she didn't want to be resurrected with only one leg. The Chief Rabbi of Israel came to her bedside and convinced her that Jewish law insists that she have the operation.

Hence, Maimonides rules that every human being – his body and his life – are owned by God (Laws of Murder 1:4); a major sixteenth-century commentary on Maimonides, Rabbenu David Ben Zimra, thereby explains the fact that although an individual is always accepted in the area of civil law when he claims he owes someone else a sum of money or a specific physical object, as the halakha declares, "the admission of the owner is equal to one hundred witnesses" – an individual is never believed when he claims that he has committed a capital crime and is therefore culpable for capital punishment. Here one dare not invoke the precedent of "the admission of the owner is equal to one hundred witnesses." The reason for the distinction: We own our money and our property; we do not own our souls. God owns our souls, our existential selves.

Rabbi S.Y. Zevin, one of the great halakhic authorities of Israel during the first decades of the State, emphasized the point we have just discussed in a fascinating article entitled "The Case of Shylock." He convincingly argues that had indeed Shylock been a religious Jewish moneylender, he could never have demanded a pound of Antonius' flesh in payment of a debt even if Antonius had agreed to that condition, Shakespeare's *Merchant of Venice* notwithstanding. After all, Antonius' body belonged neither to Shylock nor even to himself; his body and his life belonged to God.

Kedoshim

Marriage As a Loving Friendship in Sanctified Purity

> *And you shall not let any of your seed pass*
> *through (the fire) to Moloch, neither shall you*
> *profane the name of your God, I am the Lord.*
>
> LEVITICUS 18:21

The great Talmudic sage Rav Yehuda (in the name of Rav) applies the commandment "love your neighbor as [you love] yourself" to the relationship of husband and wife, the closest and most proximate of neighbors. Indeed, one of the seven blessings under the nuptial canopy even refers to the couple as *"re'im ahuvim"* or "beloved (loving) friends."

But the marriage ceremony itself, one of the most exalted and simplistically stunning in our liturgy, raises a number of problematic issues. The initial blessing of betrothal declares:

> Blessed are You, Lord our God, Sovereign of the Universe, Who has sanctified us with His commandments, commanded us

regarding forbidden sexual relationships, prohibited us from sexual relations with our fiancé and has permitted us those to whom
we are married by means of the nuptial canopy and the betrothal
sanctification. Blessed are You Who sanctifies His nation Israel
by means of the nuptial canopy and betrothal sanctification.

What makes this formulation so strikingly different from every other
blessing over a commandment is that it mentions what is forbidden as
a prelude to what it permitted. Why? Would it not have been sufficient
for the blessing to have spoken only about the positive, without mentioning the negative?

Moreover, there are an additional seven blessings recited under
the nuptial canopy which go far beyond the loving relationship of the
couple about to be wed; one blessing brings us all the way back to Adam
and Eve in the Garden of Eden ("cause these loving [and beloved]
friends to joyfully rejoice just as You caused Your creations to rejoice
in the Garden of Eden"), and the final blessing brings us forward to the
future period of redemption ("May there soon be heard in the Cities of
Judea and in the broad spaces of Jerusalem the sound of rejoicing and
the sound of happiness, the sound of grooms and the sound of brides.")
What has a marriage ceremony to do with a national history spanning
incalculable centuries from ancient past to anticipated future?

The answer is to be found in the seemingly problematic structure
of the three main chapters in the Torah portion of *Kedoshim* and part
of the previous portion of *Aḥarei Mot*. Chapter eighteen of the book of
Leviticus (the concluding chapter of *Aḥarei Mot*) deals with forbidden
sexual relationships, beginning with incest and concluding with sacrificing one's child to the idol, Moloch, and the prohibition against homo-
sexuality; chapter nineteen, which opens the portion of *Kedoshim*, starts
with the commandment to revere one's parents and then catalogues
scores of laws dealing with interpersonal relationships, including loving
one's neighbor as one loves oneself. And then, in chapter twenty, the
Bible returns to the catalogue of forbidden sexual relationships, beginning with the prohibition of sacrificing one's child to the idol, Moloch.
Why not have all the forbidden sexual relationships in one place? Why
the seeming interruption with chapter nineteen?

What is equally strange and disturbing is that the initial introduction to the laws of forbidden sexual relationships (at the beginning of chapter eighteen) is the verse: "You shall observe My decrees and My statutes which a human being shall do and live by them…" (Lev. 18:5). Our talmudic sages deduce from the command "You shall…live by them" that when push comes to shove, the Jew must generally transgress a commandment rather than forfeit his life; the value of a human life stands above the commands of the Torah (*Yoma* 85a, b). However, the sole exceptions to this rule are the three most stringent prohibitions of idolatry, sexual immorality and murder. Hence, if a Jew is ordered to commit an act of incest or adultery or else he will be murdered, he may not invoke the usual "You shall…live by them" and commit the forbidden act, but rather he must choose to die rather than to transgress. If this is the case, then how can we understand the command "You shall…live by them" placed as the introduction to the laws of sexual immorality? These are specifically the prohibitions for which a person must be willing to lay down his life.

Rabbi Mordechai Elon sees the beginning of the answer in Rashi's comment on the command "You shall live by them." Rashi explains that this injunction refers to the world to come, because if you will suggest that it refers to this world, eventually (everyone in this world) dies (Rashi, Lev. 18:5). If I might alter Rashi's words a little without removing his fundamental idea, I would suggest that it refers to life in its historical dimension, to the ability of the individual Jew to participate as a link in the great and eternal chain of Jewish historic being. The family is the bedrock of the nation, and it is specifically the laws of sexual morality which guarantee Jewish preservation and continuity physically as well as spiritually. An individual destroys his seeds of continuity if he sacrifices his child to Moloch, or if he defies the familial faithfulness by adultery. In the most profound sense, Judaism will only continue to live eternally if the laws of sexual immorality are seen as so sacrosanct that they even stand above the value of preserving a human life. Therefore, the laws of interpersonal human relationships, the necessary bedrock of a well-ordered and continuing society, must be preceded and followed by the stringent rules against sexual immorality; only then will we truly live as an eternal historic nation.

Thus the Bible, in its very chapter sequence, expresses one of the essential and amazing paradoxes of Jewish life. If the Jewish nation wishes to live as a distinct historical entity whose mission is to perfect society and redeem the world, they must first and foremost conform to the laws of family sanctity and the prohibition of sexual immorality – and this is Leviticus, chapter eighteen. Then come the fundamental principles of interhuman relationships, beginning with proper reverence for parents and including the love one must feel for one's spouse, not forgetting the prohibitions against jealousy and the commandments concerning tithes and charity for those who do not have their own property or means of livelihood – and this is chapter nineteen. The Bible then finds it necessary to return to the laws of sexual morality, the very actions which cause us to lose the succeeding generations, if not physically then certainly spiritually (as certain as giving our children over to Moloch), but this time including the capital punishments, the very antithesis of the introductory "You shall live by them," for those who actually transgress – and this is chapter twenty.

The structure and lesson of the biblical form is exquisitely maintained in the precise formulation of the marital blessings, the couple (and eventual family) representing the fundamental key to Jewish survival and eternity. The Almighty has forbidden certain sexual relationships; only if and when we maintain these prohibitions shall we have earned the unique honor of having been sanctified by means of the nuptial canopy and betrothal sanctification. And the reward for living such a sanctified life is that it enables us to live eternally as a link in the golden chain of the Jewish historical continuum – with memories which go back to the Garden of Eden and visions of anticipation which go forward to the ultimate redemption. The marriage canopy bears both the responsibility and the glory of Jewish eternity, past and future.

What Does Holiness Mean?

> *Speak unto all the congregation of the children of*
> *Israel and say to them: You shall be holy, for I the*
> *Lord your God am holy.*
>
> LEVITICUS 19:2

Holiness is certainly a "religious" word expressing a worthy ideal, if not the worthiest of all. But upon encountering this idea in the opening verses of this portion, we must admit that the concept seems rather vague and difficult to define. What does it really mean to be "holy"?

Examining some of the commentators on this issue of holiness, the remarks of Rashi and Nahmanides are thought-provoking, not only because of their differences, but also because of their similarities.

Rashi explains the phrase "you shall be holy…" as follows:

> You shall separate yourselves! Abstain from forbidden sexual rela-
> tionships and from sin, because wherever you find a warning to
> guard against sexual immoratlity, you find the mention of holiness.
> Rashi on Leviticus 19:2

Since the sexual drive is probably the strongest of our physiological needs and urges – and the most likely to get us into trouble (an old Yiddish proverb has it that most men dig their graves with their sexual organ) – it makes sense that Rashi will use this activity as a paradigm for all others. Who is a holy individual? The one who can control his sexual temptations, and arrange his life in a way in which he/she will not end up trapped in forces which often overtake and destroy all too many families.

Nahmanides, after initially quoting Rashi's understanding of holiness, goes a step further by pointing out that the rabbinic interpretation of the phrase (as cited in the *Midrash Torat Kohanim*) doesn't limit the holiness of self-restraint exclusively to sexual behavior, but rather applies it to all elements of human nature: The commandment is ordering disciplined conduct in every aspect of life!

Nahmanides goes on to explain that a Jew may punctiliously observe all the details of the laws and still act "repulsively, within the parameters of the Torah" (*naval b'reshut ha'Torah*). In effect, argues Nahmanides, the commandments must be seen as the floor of the building and not as the ceiling: everyone must keep all the laws as a minimum requirement, and then add to them as his/her personality or conscience desires or dictates, as well as in accordance with the nature of the situation which arises.

Since life is so complex, we require necessary guideposts or clearly enunciated goals to help us make the proper decisions regarding our daily conduct – especially in those areas where a black and white halakhic directive does not exist. Therefore, "you shall be holy" is the guidepost or meta-halakhic principle which must determine our relationship to the Creator. It reminds us that although drinking and eating kosher foods, for example, may be technically permitted, an individual who strives for holiness dare not spend the majority of his time in pursuit of delectable dishes and outstanding wines. And in Judaism, as Nahmanides would see it, holiness refers to a God-like personality, a person who strives to dedicate him/herself to lofty goals of compassionate and moral conduct. Self-restraint and proper balance between extremes are necessary prerequisites for a worthy human-divine relationship.

Nahmanides finds the parallel for the meta-halakhic "you shall be holy" in the human-divine relationship, within the equally meta-halakhic "you shall do what is right and good" (Deut. 6:18) in all of our interpersonal human relationships. It is impossible for the Torah to detail every single possible point of contact between two human beings, points which could easily become stressful and litigious. Thus, Nahmanides tells us that doing what is right and good must be the overall rubric under which we are to conduct our affairs.

It turns out that Rashi's focus regarding the concept of "you shall be holy" concerns matters of sexuality, while Nahmanides focuses on the entire range of our experience, giving us a global view of modesty and restrained human conduct. A formalistic reason for these two different approaches to the interpretation of holiness may derive from the context of the verse in question. Apparently, the placement of the commandment "you shall be holy" which opens chapter nineteen, sends Rashi and Nahmanides in two different directions. Rashi, finding that immediately preceding the mandate to be holy, the Torah presents all the laws of improper sexual behavior – twenty-three biblical prohibitions, twenty-three forbidden sexual alliances – he is inspired to conclude that holiness must refer first and foremost to the sexual realm.

Nahmanides, however, gazes ahead and sees, following the directive "to be holy," no less than 51 commandments in *Kedoshim* unfolding before him, with approximately half dealing with ritual and the other half dealing with the ethical – including such famous laws as "love your neighbor as yourself" and "you shall not place a stumbling block before the blind." Nahmanides therefore prefers to view holiness as applying to the entire range of the human experience.

In a most basic way, however, the two approaches are very similar. Both Rashi and Nahmanides define holiness as disciplined self-control, as the ability to say "no" to one's most instinctive physical desires. They both understand that the religious key to human conduct requires love and limits, the ability to love others and the self-control to set limits on one's desires. Today's society thinks it understands love, but it refuses to admit the necessity to set clear limits. Most advertisements try to deceive the public into thinking that everything is possible and within grasp. Therefore all products, from deodorants to underwear to jeans, feature men surrounded by adoring and seductive women. The truth –

taught especially by Rashi, but certainly seconded by Nahmanides – is that it is impossible to love in a really profound way unless one also has the ability to set limits on one's desires and actions. "Thou shalt love thy neighbor as thyself" must be limited by "thou shalt not commit adultery."

Postscript: Another Level of Holiness

What does it mean to be a Jew? Rabbi Yehezkel Abramsky, great sage and judge of London and Jerusalem, maintains that it means that you belong to a special nation, that you belong to a special religion, and that you belong to a sacred or holy community. Each of these three unique aspects of our ethnicity is expressed in a prayer recited each morning after we fall prostrate before our God (*Taḥanun*).

The prayer opens:

> Guardian of Israel, guard the remnant of Israel, and do not destroy Israel, those who recite "*Shema Yisrael.*"

The prayer speaks of Israel and not Jews, of our national heritage rather than of our religious faith. Israel is, after all, the name of our common grandfather, *Yisrael Saba*; it is the special term for our national homeland – and every family descendant responds to the familiar words *shema Yisrael*. We begin this prayer by entreating the Almighty to preserve even those Jews whose connection is merely an amorphous association with a family-state-nation, who have no real identification with a traditional code of conduct or a commitment to a particular faith or set of beliefs. It is enough that they are citizens of the State of Israel, or are even Diaspora Jews who identify with the "Jewish family" in times of crisis. This is the covenant of Jewish peoplehood which God established with Abraham. After all, did not Hitler send even those "minimalistic" Jews into the gas chambers of Auschwitz and Treblinka?

The prayer continues:

> Guardian of a unique people, guard the remnant of a unique

nation, and do not destroy a unique people, who declare Your
name one and unique, the Lord our God is one and unique.

We are now seeking to preserve those who see themselves as Jews and
not merely as Israelis, those who live a unique traditional life style of
Sabbath, festivals and kashrut, those who are committed to faith in one
God – ethical monotheism. These Jews express the covenant at Sinai,
the special religious beliefs and way of life which make Jews a singular
and unique people.

And the prayer concludes:

Guardian of a sacred people, guard the remnant of a sacred nation,
and do not destroy a sacred people, who triplicate with three
sanctities before the Sacred One.

Apparently this is the final and highest aspect of our ethnicity: in addition to our being a nation and a religion, Jews and Israelis, bound up
together with a family-nation-state and committed to a system of traditions and beliefs, we must also strive to be sacred, holy. That is the very
first command of the Torah reading of *Kedoshim*: "you shall be holy." But
we must still query, what does it mean to be holy?

The Hebrew word *kadosh* means "transcendent," above physical
blandishments and even beyond this material world, "wholly other";
within the Bible, the word "holy" generally refers to God Himself, who
is within the world but also beyond it, separate from the material world.
Who is holy? An individual who can say no to a monetary bribe or a
sexual seduction, who can give up materialistic comforts when the need
arises, who can even give up this world for the sake of external values.

Who is holy? Roi Klein, a young graduate of the yeshiva in Eli,
who loved his nation, his land and his Torah with all his heart and soul.
In the Second Lebanon war in the summer of 2006, against Hizbullah,
he found himself in Bint Jbeil removing armaments together with his
army reserve unit. He was standing near the entrance – and suddenly
realized that a Palestinian terrorist had just thrown a grenade into their
building. He thought for a split second, recited the *Shema*, and grabbed

the grenade with his hands and body. He immediately lost his life, but he saved the lives of all of his companions.

Who is holy? Yosef Goodman, son of my beloved friends Mordechai and Anne Goodman, whose parachute became entangled with the parachute of his army commander during a special training maneuver. Yosef made the holy decision; he disentangled his parachute, catapulted to certain death on the ground below, but saved the life of his commanding officer.

Please, God, preserve these holy Jews.

Yes, God, preserve these Jews who have only the most fundamental Jewish ethnic ties; preserve those Jews who have deeper Jewish religious ties; and preserve those Jews who have attained a degree of God-like holiness! Preserve all the members of the Jewish nation, for each of us has the capacity to reach up for holiness!

Post Script: Halakha as a Floor, Not a Ceiling

Is Halakha the maximum ideal toward which we strive, or the minimal expectation of conduct which is necessary for a well-ordered and ethical society? In the words of Dr. Eugene Korn (in a masterful article he wrote for *Edah*), "Is halakha a floor or a ceiling?"

Nahmanides expounds an indubitably clear position in his explanation of the commandment "you shall be holy." In answer to his query that this particular commandment appears to be too general and undefined, Nahmanides explains that despite all of the detailed laws of the Bible, it is still possible for clever and unscrupulous individuals to technically remain within the confines of the law while completely defying the spirit and goal which the laws are trying to accomplish. They can spend most of their time grossly overeating, for example, or they can continually make everyone in their company feel inferior and incapable by a cynical and supercilious manner of behavior, neither of which activity is specifically prohibited by Jewish law.

In order to prevent the creation of what Nahmanides calls "a scoundrel within the boundaries of the Torah," he maintains that there are two "meta-halakhic" overarching principles which teach us the real goal of Jewish law. These principles help us determine the correctness of a specific deed or behavior pattern which is not necessarily forbidden or obligated within the 613 commandments: (1) "You shall be holy" in the sphere of person-God relationships, and (2) "You shall do what is righteous and good" (*ve'asita hayashar vehatov*) in the sphere of interpersonal relationships. These commandments are purposefully vague and open-ended in order to leave room for right-of-conscience decisions (wherein you really know what you ought to do even though the Torah does not specifically order you to do it) as well as for changes in societal norms which certainly must affect our personal and national conduct.

For example, in a completely polygamous world, the Bible does not condemn polygamy; nevertheless, the Bible does tell us that "an individual must leave one's mother and father and cleave unto his/her spouse so that they become one flesh," certainly insinuating that the wholeness of the couple is comprised of a couple and not a *ménage a trois*. It is interesting to note that there is not one single instance of a polygamous union by any one of the sages of the Mishna, despite the biblical leniency.

A second example is the methodology of warfare, wherein the sages of the Talmud completely obviated the possibility of our "not keeping alive any man, woman or child" of the indigenous seven nations of Canaan with their setting down of the principle that "Sennacherib came and completely confounded and intermingled the nations of the world" (*Berakhot* 28b), thus making the total obliteration of the seven nations obsolete and inapplicable in later generations.

The guiding principle of the Written Law (called the "harsh law" or *dina detakfa* by the mystical *Zohar*) seems to have been that if a leader is one step ahead of his people, he is a genius, but if he is two steps ahead of his people, he is a crackpot. Hence we understand the ongoing importance of the Oral Law, continuing through our responsa literature to this very day, which the *Zohar* refers to as the "soft law" or *dina derafiya*.

Permit me to give two clear examples of where the *halakhic* code is clearly viewed by our sages not only as a minimal standard, but even as a practice which must be improved upon by anyone who wishes to be considered a good or righteous individual.

The Talmud in *Bava Metzia* 83b records an incident in which two porters transported wine barrels for Rabbah bar bar Hanan, a wealthy scholar and sage in his own right. Through an act of negligence on their part, they broke the barrels; Rabbah took their cloaks in payment for their negligence, which is what the law demands. They complained to Rav, the legal adjudicator in that area, and he instructed Rabbah to return their cloaks. "Is this the law?" asked an astonished Rabbah. "Yes," replied Rav, "based on the verse in Proverbs 2:20: 'In order that you walk in the way of the good people.'" The porters went once again to complain to Rav: "But we are hungry, since we worked all day and received no payment," whereupon Rav further instructed Rabbah to provide them with a salary as well. Once again Rabbah asked: "Is this too the law?" to which Rav replied, "Yes, in accordance with the latter half of the same verse '…and the paths of the righteous shall you observe'." Clearly, Rav was saying to Rabbah that for him – Rabbah bar bar Hanan, the wealthy scholar matched against two poverty-stricken porters – the law would expect that he would act beyond the legal requirement and provide the porters with payment for their day's labor, despite the losses they had incurred for Rabbah as a result of their negligence.

Maimonides is even clearer in his exposition: The Bible allows for gentile (Canaanite) slaves, although the Decalogue provides that the Israelites "observe the Sabbath day to keep it holy…in order that your gentile manservants and maid-servants may rest *like you*," expressing Hebrew and gentile equality before God. In his *Mishneh Torah*, Maimonides rules:

> The Israelite is permitted to work his Canaanite slave with vigor. But even though the law is such, it is a trait of piety and the way of the wise to be compassionate, to pursue righteousness and to see to it that the slave not be scorned, but is to be addressed kindly…His complaints must be seriously dealt with…After all, the book of Job teaches, "Is it not true that one stomach has formed me (the Israelite) and him (the gentile slave), and that one womb (of the One) has fashioned us both."
>
> Laws of Servants 9:8

How to Give Instruction

> You shall not hate your brother in your heart; you
> must surely instruct your colleague, so that you do
> not bear his sin.
>
> LEVITICUS 19:17

In order for an individual to be considered guilty of transgression, it is necessary that he be warned – or chastised – in advance of his crime, in order to ascertain that he is committing the forbidden deed willfully and with full understanding of the seriousness of his transgression. One of the greatest religio-legal adjudicators of the last generation, Rabbi Abraham Isaiah Karelitz (known as the Hazon Ish), courageously ruled that the Jewish community dare not condemn and ostracize disbelievers or heretics these days, because there are no longer Jewish religious models capable of properly chastising them. His proof text is a famous dictum of Rabbi Tarfon, who declared two millennia ago:

> I would marvel at meeting someone who can properly chastise. The moment one individual says to another, "Remove the flint

between your teeth" the other will respond, "How dare you chas-
tise me? You first must remove the beam from between your eyes."
Arakhin 16b

Especially in our post-modern society, where almost anything goes and
every possible moral or immoral position may be justified and rational-
ized by the subjective perspective of the individual who espouses it, it
becomes increasingly difficult for a religious leader to act as a moral
censor, chastising specific people for improper conduct. Indeed, is
there any way at all in which one can move the transgressor to see the
evil in his action?

I would like to recount some incidents which reflect two different (but complementary) methods of "chastisement" for our generation,
and the reader may decide as to their effectiveness.

The first incident is when the Chafetz Chaim took a yeshiva student who smoked on Shabbat into his home, warmly held his hand in
his own, and merely said but one word, "Shabbos," as his tears fell on
the student's hand.

The second is based on the Mussar Navardok Academy, founded
by one of the most outstanding disciples of Rabbi Yisrael Salanter, Rabbi
Yosef Yozel. One of the principles of this higher academy of Jewish learn-
ing – which emphasized individual training in character development
and had 180 Yeshivot throughout Europe before the Nazis destroyed
all but one – was "*hatava bimkon hakpada*," respect rather than resent-
ment, repay insult with heightened consideration, respond to a slap with
an embrace. The idea was that if an individual did me a bad turn, the
most effective way for him to realize the evil of his deed would be by
my behaving toward him with special accord and sensitivity. Hopefully,
the contrast would make him realize the folly of his actions.

Rabbi Nekritz, a great sage and devotee of the Navardok school of
ethical training, was marrying off a granddaughter to Rabbi Yehiel Perr.
Many of the Torah sages – rabbis, grand-rabbis and *roshei* yeshiva – were
present, many more worthy scholars than there were blessings and hon-
ors to dispense under the nuptial canopy during the ceremony. Everyone
of the assembled was greatly surprised when an unknown rabbi was given
the signal honor of intoning the last of the seven nuptial blessings, known

as *brakha aharita*. It was assumed that this relatively unknown rabbi must have had some special influence on the bride and groom – but, truth to tell, they had not laid eyes upon him before their wedding ceremony and hadn't the faintest idea who he was. Rabbi Nekritz was frequently asked that evening who his special guest was, but he responded only with a silent and knowing smile. It was only after the rabbi had passed away, and during the week of mourning in his honor, when his granddaughter herself (who had been the bride) asked her grandmother about the strange guest's identity, that the secret was revealed.

Several years before, Rabbi and Rebbetzin Nekritz had been invited to the wedding of the daughter of a rabbi they didn't really know. He kept calling and pressing them, so they agreed to attend. They assumed he would arrange transportation, but when he did not, they traveled by bus and train to the catering hall. They were seated with people they didn't know, Rabbi Nekritz was not given an honor during the ceremony, and no arrangements were made to take them home. When Rabbi Nekritz's granddaughter was married, he invited that same rabbi – and honored him with the final blessing. *Hatava bimkom hakpada* – he repaid insult with respect.

A third method of chastisement was effectuated by a well-known friend of mine, the learned and charismatic educator Rabbi Benjamin Levine – grandson of the sainted *tzaddik* of Jerusalem, Rabbi Arye Levin. He was invited a year in advance to speak at the graduation ceremony of a high school in Israel which bore the name of his sainted grandfather. A short while before the graduation, he was hospitalized with a difficult bout of pneumonia. He returned home greatly weakened – and the evening of the graduation was cold, windy and rainy. His wife called the assistant principal asking that her husband be excused due to illness. "It would be a desecration of God's name if he doesn't show up. He must come, even if he has to crawl on all fours to get here," she responded, not even offering to send (or pay for) a taxi. My friend insisted on going – despite his wife's remonstrances that he rest at home – and he set out by bus. The entire trip he thought to himself, "How would my grandfather have taught this assistant principal that she had reacted insensitively? My grandfather would have attempted to provide her with an ideal model of proper conduct."

When Rabbi Levine rose to speak, he said he had to give a brief introduction. He wanted to give a special thanks to the assistant principal, who had arranged for him to speak. He said that when she heard he had been ill with pneumonia, she called to graciously suggest that perhaps in light of the inclement weather he ought to stay at home. When he said that he felt he had to come under any condition, she offered to send a taxi. He felt it only proper to thank her for her sensitivity and consideration before giving his commencement address. The audience gave the assistant principal a standing ovation. She called my friend the next day to apologize and to thank him for having taught her a most important lesson.

Who is the Neighbor We Must Love Like Ourselves?

You shall not avenge, nor bear any grudge against the children of your people, but you shall love your neighbor like yourself, I am the Lord

LEVITICUS 19:18

If there is one commandment from among the 613 which stands out as the shining example of biblical morality and as the quintessence of the Jewish contribution to universal ethics, it is "You shall love your neighbor like yourself." Such is the ringing declaration of one of the greatest interpreters of Torah in all of our history, Rabbi Akiva, who taught: "You shall love your neighbor 'like yourself' – this is the great[est] principle of the Torah" (Yerushalmi *Nedarim* 9:4).

But precisely because this commandment is so significant, it is crucial that it be properly understood. If indeed it is an ethical commandment dealing with interpersonal relationships, why does the verse conclude, "I am the Lord." What does God have to do with it? And is it really possible for one to truly love another like he/she loves him/ herself – or is this a totally unrealistic expectation? And precisely who is the "neighbor" (*re'a*) of whom the Bible speaks? Is it limited to some-one who lives in your town, or to a fellow religionist, or to an observant Jew – or is it universally inclusive of every human being? It seems to me that the answer to these questions, as well as the precise application of the commandment in our day-to-day affairs, will speak volumes as to the nature of Judaism itself as a world religion.

I would argue that the concluding words of the verse, "I am the Lord," are the real key to our proper interpretation of the commandment itself. The Bible opens with the proclamation that "In the beginning God created the heavens and the earth" (Gen. 1:1] and goes on to describe the divine creation of all living things, up to and including the human being created in the divine image. The book of Exodus then speaks of the God of the exodus as the Lord Redeemer who took the Israelites out of Egypt (*"I am the Lord* who took you out of Egypt, the house of bondage" [Ex. 20:2]). These two towering biblical events, both effectu-ated exclusively by God, are the defining building blocks of our Jewish faith: Our elaborate system of blessings and prayers hark back to God as the Creator of world and life, and our traditional festivals and ritu-als are in large measure a reminder of the exodus from Egypt. What is less frequently noted, however, is that these two cataclysmic events are both dramatically interrelated – and also serve as the foundation of our ethical interpersonal relationships.

If the Lord is Creator, then all human beings are creatures; it then follows logically that one creature dare not "lord" it over any other crea-ture. To do so would be usurping the exclusive place of the divine! If the Lord is parent-in-heaven, we are all siblings in this amazingly heteroge-neous planet which is becoming a global village; it then follows logically that one sibling dare not harm or take advantage of another sibling. The Creator-Lord or parenthood of God demands the fundamental equal-ity – and freedom under God – of every human being. And so the God of creation had to also emerge as the God of the exodus – the God who had to teach every despotic tyrant that there is absolutely no justifica-tion for enslaving other human beings. And so Rabbi Abraham Ibn Ezra interprets our verse, "You shall love your neighbor like yourself, I am the Lord," to mean that since I am the Lord who created every human being equally, as one, you must love each other as you love yourselves.

Let us explore the word *re'a* a bit further, and we will appreciate the words of Ibn Ezra with even greater depth. Rabbi David Shmuel Pardo in his commentary *Maskil LeDavid* proposes that the word *re'akha* in our verse also includes God. He refers to Hillel's response to the would-be proselyte (*Shabbat* 31), "What is hateful to you, do not do to your friend," wherein Rashi cites a verse in Proverbs 27:10, "Do not forsake your own friend and your father's friend – *re'a*," a clear reference to God, the "friend" of all generations. *Re'a* can likewise mean the whole historic Israel, as it is used in the Song of Songs (4:1 and throughout). And of course, the Ibn Ezra has said that *re'a* means the whole of humanity. Rabbi Yitzhak Hutner ingeniously suggests that *re'a* comes from the same root word as *terua*, the broken (*ra'a*) sound of the shofar. What is the connection between all that we have said and brokenness?

A Hassidic tale of two beloved friends, the Treske and the Voorker, who studied together in the yeshiva from early childhood into young adulthood, will explain. When they had to leave the yeshiva and part ways – each to his destiny as a religious leader – each one decided to take leave of his friend with a photograph of the other. At their moment of parting, however, they tore each photograph in half, leaving each with half a photograph of himself and half a photograph of the other. The message was: one friend without the other is only half an individual. And so it is on every level: An individual without his friend is a broken person; the Jewish nation disunited and bereft of some of its people is a broken nation; humanity torn apart by strife and hatred is a shattered world; and the Almighty separated from His creations is exiled, and becomes the most tragic expression of a cosmos filled with broken vessels.

Only when friends, Jews and human beings unite with God and with each other will God become one, will His world become one, and will peace and redemption reign supreme. Each of us remains a broken shard without all of the rest.

Hence I believe that the most accurate interpretation of our commandment must be: "You shall love your neighbor *because* he is [a human being] like you; I am the Lord who made and resides within all of you." We are all part of the same one, each broken without the other.

How do we express this fundamental principle in our daily activities? Hillel the Elder maintained the commandment is to be observed more by what we refrain from doing than by what we actually do. When a would-be proselyte came before the sage asking to be converted on the condition that he be taught the entire Torah while standing on one leg, Hillel responded: "What is hateful to you, do not do to your friend. This is the entire Torah; the rest is interpretation, which you must go and learn" (*Shabbat* 31a). Nahmanides (ad loc.) reads this commentary into the very prefix "*l*" of the biblical "*l're'akha*," literally "you shall love *towards* your friend"; act toward him as if you loved him like yourself by not doing to him what you would consider hateful if done to you.

Martin Buber utilizes the strange prefix form "*l*" (*lamed*) of the biblical text to establish a fundamental principle of human relationships – and at the same time strengthen the theological underpinning with which we began our discussion (Buber, *I and Thou*). We would have expected to find the biblical phrase, "you shall love *et reakha*," the conjunctive *et* always appearing before an objective case; in this context, "you shall love" is the subject and "your friend" is the object. A human being is never to be seen as an object, thunders Buber. A fellow human being is never *acted upon*; he must always be *related to* (*l're'akha*). When we use another human being merely as a means to our end, not recognizing him/her as a child of God in the fullness of his/her being, we are establishing an illegitimate "I-it" relationship rather than the biblically mandated "I-thou" relationship. Using another, taking advantage of the other, robbing another of his/her freedom of choice and independent development – even if they be family members or students – are all forms of slavery which must be prohibited. "You must act with love toward your neighbor in the fullness of a relationship of equals, because he/she is like you, under God the Creator who demands universal freedom."

From this perspective, it would be indubitably clear that in accordance with Ibn Ezra, Tosafot Yom Tov, and Rabbi Hayim Vital, "your neighbor" in this context includes a gentile as well. After all, the text does not read "your brother" or "your colleague" (as it does earlier); indeed, the etymology of *re'a* (neighbor or friend) may even include someone who may be evil (*ra*), but certainly someone who may differ from you in looks, ethnic origins or ideology. Does not the Bible similarly explain the Sabbath day "in order that your gentile manservant and maidservant may rest *like you*" (*kamokha*, because he/she is like you, [Deut. 5:13]), utilizing the same *kamokha* as in our verse to specifically refer to a gentile! Furthermore, it would seem that the universal application of this commandment, as well of the entire Torah, is the precise point of Ben Azzai's addition to Rabbi Akiva's words:

> Rabbi Akiva says, "You shall love your neighbor like yourself," – this is the great[est] principle of the Torah. Says Ben Azzai, "This is the book of generations of humanity (Gen. 5:1) – that is an even greater principle!"
>
> *Sifra Kedoshim*, Chap. 2

Ben Azzai is reminding us that every human being contains the essential spark of the one God, who created us all as one!

Postscript

One of the ironies of the life and teachings of Rabbi Akiva is that this very same commandment, which for him was apparently so cardinal, came back to haunt him. The Talmud records that between the period of Passover and Lag Ba'Omer (fifteen days before Shavuot), twelve thousand pairs of Rabbi Akiva's disciples died; indeed, it is because of their death that these weeks have become a season of semi-mourning for observant Jews, with weddings, haircuts and group festivities absolutely forbidden at this time. And when the Talmudic sages query as to *why* such Torah scholars met such a premature demise during such a concentrated period, the response is "because they did not treat each other with proper respect"; in other words, they did not properly keep the commandment to love your neighbor like yourself (*Yevamot* 62b)! Could it be that the great master's disciples failed to internalize the major teaching of their rebbe? If indeed Rabbi Akiva began to emphasize this commandment only after the tragedy befell his students, it may be understandable; but it is difficult to imagine that such a Torah giant would have grasped the central significance of this cardinal command-ment only at the end of his life!

I believe that the answer to the mystery may be found on a deeper examination of the circumstances surrounding the death of the twenty-four thousand students. After the Talmud records the time frame of their demise – from Passover until fifteen days before Shavuot – Rabbi Nahman adds that the immediate cause of their death was *"askera,"* a for-eign word which Rashi defines as diphtheria-whooping cough, a plague (*Yevamot* ibid). However, we have no corroborating evidence, either from a parallel Talmudic passage or from the Second Commonwealth historian Josephus, that a plague broke out at this time; moreover, it is difficult to imagine a malady which only affected the students of one particular master!

Rav Hai Gaon maintains that Rabbi Akiva's twenty-four thou-sand students were killed not in a plague but rather in the Bar Kochba rebellion and its aftermath, the Hadrianic Persecutions, which he calls *shmada*. Approximately sixty-five years after the destruction of the Second Temple at the hands of the Roman government, Rabbi Akiva accepted the possibility that Shimon bar Kochba was the long-awaited Messiah-King of Jewish redemption, and urged the Judeans to wage a war of independence against Rome; indeed, he organized what was in effect the first Yeshivat Hesder in history. It makes eminently good sense that in the massive defeat of Bar Kochba's legions, twenty-four thousand of Rabbi Akiva's disciples lost their lives. It is also quite possible that Rabbi Nahman's *askera* might come from the Greek *sicarii*, which means "by the sword"! Hence, it was not a plague but rather a war of independence against Rome that claimed the lives of so many of Rabbi Akiva's students.

There remains one more piece to this puzzle. Rabbi Yohanan ben Zakai was the teacher of the two main teachers of Rabbi Akiva, Rabbi Yehoshua and Rabbi Eliezer – and Rabbi Yohanan ben Zakai had pre-scribed accommodation with Rome sixty-five years earlier just prior to the Temple's destruction. Indeed, it was Rabbi Yohanan ben Zakai who went out to meet Vespasian, the Roman general, and made the deal of giving up Jerusalem in return for the city of Yavneh and her wise men (*Sanhedrin*).

One version of the Talmud records that Rabbi Akiva vehemently disagreed with the "dovish"' approach of his rebbe; the disciple is even cited as having criticized his teacher by quoting a prophetic verse which he claimed referred to Rabbi Yohanan:

> Sometimes wise men are turned backward and their wisdom is transformed into foolishness.
>
> Isaiah 44:25

Undoubtedly, Rabbi Akiva was a great idealist who believed passionately in Jewish national sovereignty over Israel and Jerusalem, and especially in the holy Temple, whose goal was to gather all nations of the world and inspire them to accept a God of love and peace (Isaiah 2; Micah 4). But – at least according to this version of the Talmud – the heat of the moment caused him to speak in less than respectful terms concerning a leading Jewish scholar, the teacher of his foremost teachers. Can it be that Rabbi Akiva's own disciples learned not from what their rabbi taught as much as from what their rabbi said – and so they too did not speak respectfully to each other, especially when they had differing political views even among themselves. We see from here the awesome responsibility of a rebbe. And we also see how the beginning of the end of any national uprising or even defensive war is when the people supposedly on the same side deflect their energy away from the enemy and toward their own internal dissensions: This is the causeless hatred which has always caused Israel to miss our chance for redemption!

Emor

Kohen, Rabbi, Educator: A Proper, If Difficult, Job Description

> *And the Lord said to Moses, Speak to the priests,*
> *the sons of Aaron, and say to them...*
>
> LEVITICUS 21:1

What is the major task of a religious leader, a community rabbi or the dean of a day school? This is a question that plagues every search committee as well as every practicing "professional" religionist, because, while satisfying everyone's desires and expectations is a virtual impossibility, establishing priorities and setting clear goals is an absolute necessity. We will attempt to provide some general direction derived from the priestly functions described in this Torah and *haftara* reading, bearing in mind Rabbi Yisrael Salanter's adage that if everyone is satisfied, you are not a proper rabbi, and if no one is satisfied, you are not a proper *mentsch* (sensitive human being).

The Kohen was the priest-educator during the biblical and Temple periods. The very first – and unique – commandment concerning him is that he not defile himself by contact with the dead; this is an especially telling limitation when we remember that the primary responsibility of priests of all religions is to aid their adherents to "get to the other world" – that the Bible of ancient Egypt was called the *Book of the Dead.* In effect, the Torah is teaching us that our religious leadership must deal with the living and not the dead: must spend its time teaching Torah and accessing Jewish experiences, rather than giving eulogies and visiting cemeteries; must be dedicated primarily to this world rather than the world-to-come.

Second, the high priest (*kohen gadol*) wore a head-plate upon which was written "holy unto God" and a breast-plate upon which were engraved the twelve tribes of Israel. I believe that the symbolism is quite clear: The religious leader must dedicate his mind to the divine and his heart to his people; his thoughts, plans and machinations must always be purely in line with the God-endowed principles of ethical conduct, and his feelings must be informed with love, concern and commitment to the welfare of each and every Jew. His primary task must be not so much to elevate himself to God as it is to bring God to his people; and the unique characteristics of each of the twelve tribes remind him that there are at least twelve different gates through which the divine can be sought after and encountered. The true leader helps many different individuals discover his/her pathway within Torah, his/her roadway to approach God's tent.

Third, the prophet Ezekiel (44:24) adds a phrase which we read in the *haftara* but which is based on many biblical verses: "And my directions (*torot*) and my statutes, all of my festivals, shall they *guard* (*yishmor*)." The Bible as well as our liturgy is replete with the necessity to "guard" the Torah and its commandments; from a linguistic perspective, it is fairly easy to understand the necessity to *study* Torah and *perform* the commandments, but whence comes the notion of *guarding* Torah and commandments? What does this verb *shamor* (to guard – usually mistranslated as to observe) actually mean in context?

There is a well-known midrash, cited in the Jerusalem Talmud, that Rav Ashi visited a Jewish town for the first time and asked to see the "guardians of the city" (*neturei karta*). When the townsmen brought out the policemen and firemen, the rabbinical sage rejected them; the true guardians, he insisted were the teachers of the children in the city.

The analogy goes much deeper. In the realm of torts, or civil monetary law, the Bible (Exodus 22:6–14) and the Talmud (Tractate *Bava Metzia*) delineate four prototypical guardians (*shomrim*), and the extent of their respective responsibility for the objects in their custody for safekeeping. First and foremost, they must understand that while the object may have been placed in their possession to guard for a certain period – if the owner was going on vacation, for example – the guardian dare not use it up in any way; much the opposite, the guardian or *shomer* must restore it, whole and intact, to its true and initial owner. Consequently, if the rabbi and educator is entrusted with "guarding Torah," the guardian or *shomer Torah* must understand that although the teaching is in his/her possession, its ultimate owner is God; in effect, the Almighty has deposited it as a sacred trust with the religious leaders of the community. Thus, this Torah dare not be altered or compromised; it is to be transmitted but not transmuted, taught but not tampered with. To be sure, the Torah may be interpreted and applied within the accepted rules of explication, but only by those qualified to do so and only in accordance with its own rules and regulations.

Now the analogy may be taken still further. In the realm of torts, there are those guardians who receive no payment for their guardianship (*shomer hinam*), and they are only responsible for willful neglect (*peshiya*). Similarly, there are Torah scholars who teach gratis, for the sake of the "*mitzva*." However, since the Torah itself commands that "you shall be involved therein by day and by night," (Joshua 1:8), one might legitimately argue that if a Torah guardian made himself "unavailable" when needed by a fellow Jew, whatever time it may have been by day or by night, he may well be guilty of neglect! A true guardian of Torah must understand that he/she must always be "on call" to properly dispense the obligation of the guardianship.

The guardians who *do* receive payment (*shomrei sakhar*) have a heightened responsibility in Jewish civil law: not only are they culpable of willful neglect, but they are also culpable if the object in their custody is lost or stolen. Continuing our analogy to Torah, a "professional"

Jewish leader cannot escape the tragic truth that our Torah is being lost to countless Jews who have never ever been exposed to the rich treasures of their tradition. Jewish ignorance which leads to assimilation is an advanced stage of Jewish Alzheimer's, a dreadful case of "losing it" – "it" being the essence of our history, the very bedrock of tradition upon which our future must be built. The guardians of Torah must tirelessly pursue the initiation and implementation of ideas such as "Birthright" and the creation of Jewish institutions such as outreach synagogues, day schools, summer camps, and seminars which can restore the lost treasure to its rightful owners, the Jewish people. And even if false ideologies and perversions attempt to "steal" the true Torah – such as Jews for Jesus or other Christian missionary movements attempting to capture Jews under false pretenses – it is incumbent upon the guardians of Torah to prove the falseness of such claims and to restore the pure traditions to their rightful owners.

However, it is the third level of guardianship, the borrower (*sho'el*), who is the most analogous to our Jewish leadership. In the realm of Jewish civil law, one who borrows an object for his/her own use while it is in his/her possession assumes responsibility not only for willful neglect, loss or thievery, but even for unforeseen tragedies which may threaten the existence of the object, such as fire or flood (*onsin*). Our tradition is replete with Torah teachers who continued to transmit this message, to impart their sacred trust under the most tragic of circumstances: Rabbi Akiva, who taught Torah while in prison and even while being tortured to death with iron combs under the Hadrianic persecutions; Maimonides, who continued to study, teach and write while fleeing the Almohad Muslim persecutors; Rabbi Oshry who answered religious questions and gave religious direction in the midst of the horrors of the concentration camps.

And the necessity to "guard" the Torah even under what seem to be impossible conditions may well be considered our legitimate responsibility – because Torah teachers themselves certainly use, or "borrow," their subject matter every day for personal satisfaction and enjoyment in addition to the times when they are involved in transmitting it, or restoring it to others. Indeed, the heroic activities of transplanting Torah in alien environments, the many rabbis and teachers who must organize, direct the efforts to build and fundraise for a synagogue or day school it, or to maintain teachers' wages and student lunches, are all involved in discharging this almost impossibly difficult and thankless responsibility of the guardian-borrower.

The examples of such heroic guardians of Torah are legion, even in our times. Rabbi Aharon Kotler, the fiery and uncompromising Torah giant who felt that he was snatched from the claws of the Holocaust only in order to recreate the European Torah model in America, would never take any of his students along with himself on his frequent fundraising missions on behalf of the Lakewood Yeshiva: "I want my students to also build institutions of Torah, he would say, and so I don't want them to become discouraged when they see the degradations (*bizyonot*) I must suffer."

During the three summers I spent with my family in Miami Beach, Florida in the early 1970s, I got to know, appreciate and love Rabbi Sender Gross, of blessed memory, the founder and dean of the Hebrew Academy of Miami Beach, the individual who is credited as being the pioneer who first brought Torah to Florida. I learned from him, up close, what it really means to be a Torah-guardian and to discharge one's responsibility with total dedication, completely devoid of self-interest or self-aggrandizement. Two incidents I witnessed personally: When the yeshiva high school he had started was in danger of closing because of lack of funds, and when all of its fundraising efforts proved unsuccessful, he took out a personal mortgage on his home in order to keep the yeshiva going; and at the end of his life, when the school bus drivers went on strike, he personally picked up the students and drove them to the Hebrew Academy so that their Torah study would not be interrupted. Such is the dedication of a true Torah guardian, who understands that his responsibility is not only to teach Torah to those interested in hearing it, but it is rather to preserve Torah, to transmit and instill it within the hearts and minds of the next generation, no matter how insurmountable the obstacles for doing so may appear to be. And our sages guarantee that in accordance with the commitment will come the ultimate reward.

Job Description Revisited

> *And he who is the high priest among his brethren,*
> *upon whose head the anointing oil was poured,*
> *and who is consecrated to put on the garments,*
> *shall not suffer the hair of his head to grow long,*
> *nor rend his clothes.*

LEVITICUS 21:10

In my previous commentary, I attempted to suggest a number of guidelines for the rabbi-educator, stressing his role as Torah guardian.

In 1972, in his eulogy for his revered *meḥutan* Rabbi Meshullam Zusha Twersky, the Talner Rebbe, Rabbi Joseph B. Soloveitchik clarified dual and complementary roles of religious leadership. He provided two prototypical models, the majestic *rav* and the holy *rebbe*. The majestic *rav* is essentially concerned with his students' cerebral capacities, uses the logical word as his medium of communication, and speaks to the intellectual elite; the holy *rebbe* is essentially concerned with his students' emotional capacities, uses religious experience as his medium of communication, and attempts to make contact with the soul of every single

Jew. The majestic *rav* seeks and demands exacting truth; the holy *rebbe* expresses and emanates unconditional love. The majestic *rav* chastises the one who commits a transgression with harsh words of condemnation; the holy *rebbe* weeps over one who commits a transgression and always extends his hand in forgiveness, his arm in embrace. The majestic *rav* analyzes the expressed concepts of the pages of Torah and affects the external activities of his students; the holy *rebbe* delves into the secret depths of Torah and transforms the inner world of his adherents.

The majestic *rav* is embodied in the head-plate, *tzitz*, (which contains the words: "holy unto the Lord"), while the holy *rebbe* is embodied in the breast-plate – *hoshen* – whereon were engraved the twelve tribes of Israel.

Rabbi Soloveitchik, however, revels in the glory of the dialectic, generally attempting to join together the two prototypes he often provides. Adam One and Adam Two, for example, in *The Lonely Man of Faith*, must find their proper balance in the heart and soul of the individual. And although a *rav* is known by that title of respect to the outside world, he is affectionately called *rebbe* by each of his close student followers. I would argue that both the head-plate and the breast-plate, as well as the requisite Torah qualities of leadership they represent, must be worn by the truly great religious leader of today – together in a sacred synthesis.

In another one of Rabbi Soloveitchik's essays, he extrapolates necessary qualities of religious leadership from a detailed exposition of a verse found in the prophetic reading (*haftara*) of this Torah portion:

> The priestly Levite sons of Zadok draw near to Me to serve Me…. They instruct My nation as to [their proper conduct] in distinguishing between the holy and the profane, they inform [educate] as to the difference between the pure and the impure; they bring all arguments before the bar of justice; they guard the statutes concerning all My festivals; and they cause My Sabbaths to be made holy.
>
> Ezekiel 44:15–24

Each of these priestly (or rabbinical) functions requires careful understanding and training. First of all, the authentic religious leader is a religious instructor, an adjudicator (*posek*); he must have the requisite knowledge and training to decide what is permissible from the halakhic perspective. It goes without saying that in addition to wide erudition he must have deep humility; as important as it may be to know how to *pasken* (halakhically instruct), it is even more important not to be embarrassed about admitting the complexity of the issue and consulting a higher authority.

Second, the religious leader must be a gifted educator, able to reveal before his congregant-students the internal beauty, logic and relevance of both the written and oral Torah. His command of the theoretical and conceptual aspects of Torah must be of such a caliber that he always enhances the respect in which our traditional texts are held in the minds of his listeners.

Third, the religious teacher-rabbi must be a paragon of honesty and justice, resolving conflicts with equity and discernment, clearly standing above personal gain and subjective involvement. In the words of Maimonides,

> He must fill the world [or community] with righteousness and break the arms of the wicked when he battles the wars of the Lord.
> *Mishneh Torah*, Laws of Kings 4:10

Rabbi Joseph B. Soloveitchik records in *Ish Hahalakha* how his grandfather, Rabbi Haim of Brisk, stopped the funeral of a wealthy individual on a Friday morning, insisting that since the poor person had died first, his funeral must precede that of his wealthy townsman. Indeed, Rabbi Moshe (Rabbi Joseph B. Soloveitchik's father) composed the sole words inscribed on Rabbi Haim's tombstone: "Here is buried Rabbi Haim, son of Rabbi Yosef Dov Halevi, replete with loving-kindness (*rav ḥesed*)." This quality of the fearless pursuit of justice and kindness is for Rabbi Soloveitchik the major quality of the religious teacher-rabbi.

Fourth, the religious leader must guard our religious institutions by making certain – through teaching the young and establishing the proper Torah academies – that they will continue into the next generation. He must assume the obligations of a guardian-borrower, who takes total responsibility for the sacred trust which he guards for eternity.

And, finally, the religious teacher-rabbi must ensure the sacredness of our rituals and festivals. He can only do so by being himself a model of sacred conduct, by being above reproach in his appearance and comportment at all times.

I do not suggest that Rabbi Soloveitchik's guidelines be adopted by every synagogue or day-school search committee; if they are, I'm afraid many positions of Jewish leadership will remain vacant. I do believe that they pose an important and necessary challenge to all of those who labor in the vineyard of the Lord – and we can only strive to become worthy of our calling.

What We Are Willing to Die For Will Teach Us What to Live For

> *You shall not profane My holy name: I shall be sanctified in the midst of the children of Israel. I am the Lord who sanctifies you.*
>
> LEVITICUS 22:32

During the period known as "the second intifada," mortar shells were fired at 11:30 PM onto the "caravan campus" of Yeshivat Siah Yitzhak, the *hesder* yeshiva of Ohr Torah Stone on the northern end of Efrat, bordering on Bethlehem and El Khader. The yeshiva community (comprised of some forty singles and fifteen young families) was used to gunshots and even fire-bombs; the mortar shells signaled a serious escalation. I immediately dispatched a bullet-proof van to evacuate the area and transport everyone to our Retreat Center, in a much safer place in the center of Efrat. When I checked thirty minutes later, only the women and children had arrived. "We took a vote," explained the director of the campus, "and unanimously decided that only the women and children would leave our hill. We dare not even appear to grant only a temporary victory to the enemy."

From whence is the source of this very special courage, an inner strength which has surfaced again and again in Efrat and throughout Israel? After all, despite daily drive-by shootings and terrorist suicide attacks which have caused just about everyone to attend an inordinate number of funerals and to be stricken with the anguished suffering of widows, orphans and bereaved parents, our citizens continue to face their daily lives of professional commitments and family celebrations with resolute resilience and firm faith!

I believe that an important part of the answer is to be found in a crucial commandment in the Torah portion of *Emor*: "You shall not profane My holy name: I shall be sanctified in the midst of the children of Israel. I am the Lord who sanctifies you" (Lev. 22:32). The sages of the Talmud explain "profaning the divine name" as when a rabbinic sage takes meat from a butcher without making immediate payment, or when a learned Jew is lax in his business ethics or does not speak kindly to the people at large (*Yoma* 66a). And similarly, if a sage is careful about his actions, always speaking kindly to every human being, accepting everyone cheerfully and taking precise care concerning his business ethics to the point that everyone praises him and strives to emulate his comportment, then that individual is sanctifying God's name, and about him it is said:

> And He says to me, "you are my servant Israel, through whom I am glorified."
> *Mishneh Torah*, Laws of the Foundations of Torah 5:11

This interpretation, which sees the application of the command to sanctify the Almighty as performing commandments (especially in the realm of human interpersonal relationships) in a manner which will inspire others to wish to emulate one's deeds, is very much in line with the biblical context of the verse:

> An ox or a lamb; you shall not slaughter an animal and its offspring on the same day.... And you shall observe My commandments

and do them, I am the Lord. You shall not profane My holy name; I shall be sanctified in the midst of the children of Israel; I am the Lord who sanctified you. [I am] He who took you out of the land of Egypt to be for you for a Lord. I am God.

Leviticus 22:28–33

However, Rashi has another interpretation – in truth the primary interpretation according to the majority of our sages:

…What is the meaning of the verse "I shall be sanctified"? Commit your lives and sanctify My name… And when an individual commits him/herself, he/she must become committed even to the point of death.

Rashi, Leviticus 22:32

Maimonides likewise interprets this commandment as follows:

And the matter of this commandment to sanctify God's name is to publicize this true faith in the world, and that we not be afraid of any harm or damage…When Nebuchadnezzar the Wicked commanded obeisance to an idol, and the multitudes of Israel bowed down to it – since there was no one to sanctify God's name because they were afraid – this was a shame and an embarrassment to all of Israel that this commandment [of sanctifying God's name] should be lost to them…

Maimonides, *Sefer HaMitzvot*,
Positive Commandment 9

In effect, Maimonides is saying that the First Temple was destroyed by Nebuchadnezzar because all of Israel were afraid to perform the commandment of martyrdom, to sacrifice their lives for their faith by refusing to worship idols!

A deeper insight into these words of Rashi and Maimonides becomes evident when we ponder another biblical anomaly just a few chapters earlier. We have previously commented on the command, "You shall observe my statutes and my commandments which a human being shall perform; and you shall live by them" (Lev. 18:5). Our sages deduce from these words: "'You shall live by them' – and not die by them." And in general, a human life takes precedence over the commandments of the Torah (Maimonides, *Mishneh Torah*, Laws of the Foundations of Torah 5:1). But then is it not strange that "You shall live by them" comes as an introduction to the laws of sexual immorality, for which you must die rather than transgress them!

I previously provided a response to this question, but now I would suggest a different answer most relevant to our Israel experience. For Judaism, it is not only an unreflected life which is of little value; a life lived for no higher value other than to keep on living is also of little value. After all, no one lives forever, hence the individual whose highest purpose in life is to go on living is someday doomed to failure! Therefore, the Torah is teaching us that we must live our lives against the backdrop of values which are more significant than any single individual life. Paradoxically, only a person who has values for which he would sacrifice his future, will merit a future; such an individual may lose his life, but he gains eternity.

Israel is now embarked on a continuation of her War of Independence in a life-and-death struggle against an enemy that still refuses to recognize our right to exist as a Jewish state in the Middle East.

We in Israel, especially in the wake of the return of European anti-Semitism, understand the crucial importance of the State of Israel for the Jewish future. For us, it is a great privilege to stand in the front lines of battle at such a fateful hour!

Martyrdom For the Sake of a Shoelace?

> *You shall not profane My holy name: I shall be*
> *sanctified in the midst of the children of Israel. I*
> *am the Lord who sanctifies you.*
>
> LEVITICUS 22:32

We have already commented on how our Talmudic sages derive from this verse the necessity of sacrificing one's life – sanctifying the name of God (*Kiddush Hashem*) – for the sake of the commandments of the Bible: Under all circumstances an individual Jew must give up his life rather than transgress any of the three major prohibitions of murder, sexual immorality or adultery. However, the Talmud does nevertheless insist that in times of gentile persecution of the Jews, a Jew must die rather than publicly transgress even the simplest, or most "minor," of Jewish laws, even a Jewish custom referring to our shoelaces (*Sanhedrin* 74a, b).

Our Talmudic sages go so far as to insist that when Jews are not being persecuted, it is forbidden for a Jew to give up his life in order not to desecrate the Sabbath, arguing that it "is better that he desecrate one Sabbath and remain alive to keep many Sabbaths."

But then how can we justify martyrdom – even if only during periods of persecution – for the sake of a Jewish custom referring to our shoelaces? What can there possibly be about a shoelace which strikes at the heart and essence of our Jewish mission?

The Ba'alei HaTosafot, the Talmudic commentaries of the Ashkenazi sages of the eleventh–twelfth centuries, when many Jews were martyred by the Crusaders, suggest that the general custom in Rome and its numerous colonies during the 2nd century was to wear white shoelaces; the Jews, however, wore black shoelaces, as a memorial to the loss of our holy Temple and the disappearance of Jewish national sovereignty in Jerusalem. When gentiles in times of persecution attempted to force Jews to wear white shoelaces – and thereby force the Jewish community to cease their mourning for the loss of our national homeland – the Jew must respond with martyrdom (*Sanhedrin* 74b, *Tosafot* ad loc).

Rabbi Joseph B. Soloveitchik added one crucial point. Among the many Jewish laws, decrees and customs which have developed from biblical times to the present, the Jews themselves do not always realize which are truly vital for our national and religious preservation; the gentiles who are persecuting us always do, because they – wishing to destroy us – strike at the jugular. Hence whatever they insist we abandon, we must maintain even at the price of our lives!

From this perspective, it becomes easier to understand why the current claws of anti-Semitism – especially throughout Europe – are expressing themselves in acts of persecution specifically focused against the State of Israel and its policies.

The gentile world, post-Holocaust, understands only too well the crucial role the State of Israel plays in Jewish survival; and Jerusalem is also the throne of our mission for world salvation, by means of universal acceptance of a God desirous of morality and peace. Any nation hell-bent on global domination through jihadic force and persecution of all dissenting opinions must oppose with all its strength the vision and presence of a Jewish Israel and Jerusalem.

Justifying Martyrdom

And you shall not profane My holy name, I shall be sanctified among the children of Israel. I am God who sanctifies you.

LEVITICUS 22:32

Giving up one's life for the sake of one's God or one's religious belief evokes images of fanatic warriors waging a jihad or of cruel suicide bombers destroying scores of innocent people in the wake of their martyrdom. One would hardly ascribe to our temperate and rational Judaism a commandment which makes the giving up of one's life – particularly the lives of our children – mandatory under certain conditions. But such is the generally given interpretation of a verse found in this Torah portion, which declares that the sanctification of God will come from the children of Israel (Lev. 22:32). As Rashi explains:

> What is the significance of the scriptural mandate "I [the Lord] must be sanctified?" Surrender your life and sanctify My name.

How can we understand such an extreme demand by the God of compassion?

We, the people of Israel, are often referred to in the Bible as "*adat hashem*," the congregation – or more literally correct, the witnesses – of the Lord. It is our mission to see to it that God is manifest in the world, that His Divine Presence is felt in the society around us. Since God is biblically defined as "Compassionate, Tolerant, Full of Loving-Kindness and Truth" (Ex. 34:6), the best way to make His presence known is by fostering acts of compassion, tolerance, loving-kindness and truth. And indeed, the High Holy Day Amida prayer declares that "the holy Lord is sanctified by righteous deeds, by acts of charity-*tzedaka*." Maimonides describes and defines the highest fulfillment of sanctifying God's name when a Torah scholar "speaks softly and kindly to all creatures. And receives everyone with warmth … and respects even those who denigrate him and comports his business dealing in good faith …. Behold [such an individual] sanctifies God's name, and about him does Scripture record 'You are My servant, Israel, through whom I am glorified.'" (Laws of the Foundations of Torah 5:10).

This is a wonderful way to sanctify God's name in a positive fashion. However, there are certain moments when extreme evil acts are being perpetrated which drive God and holiness from the world – and the individual who understands the desecration is powerless to prevent it; he may even be forced to participate in such evil as happened to many collaborators in Nazi Germany and Soviet Russia. In such instances, the Torah demands that the only way God can remain in the world is by the good people refusing to cooperate with the evil – even if they are to be killed as a result, even if their children are to be killed as a result. This is the tragic necessity: At times, to fulfill the command to sanctify God's name in a negative way, as cited by Rashi in his comments on the biblical words: "I must be sanctified among the children of Israel" quoted above and as confirmed by Maimonides (Laws of the Foundations of Torah 5:1–2(, and the *Sefer HaHinukh* (Positive Commandment 296).

There is a clear and obvious distinction between this command and the jihad-suicide bomber terrorism of fanatic fundamentalists. The Torah does not allow us to *initiate* our dying on behalf of God. We are permitted, even commanded, to do so *only* in the case of a war fought in self-defense (Maimonides, Laws of Kings 5:1, 4); since Sennacherib confounded the nations, only a war in self-defense is now relevant in an obligatory war – *milhemet mitzva* – or when the enemy compels us to worship idols (give up our ethical monotheism), to murder someone else, to rape someone else, all under penalty of death; that it is to say, if the enemy says, murder him or I'll murder you. God is the essence of morality and reverence for life. If we cooperate with those who are destroying morality and reverence for life, then we are helping to banish God and godliness from the world. In such instances, we must give up our lives rather than allow such evil to triumph. Had such been the ethical comportment of the Germans in the period of the Nazis, or of the Communists in the period of Stalin, all of history would be different, and countless lives would have been saved. No one can allow him or herself to be an accomplice to consummate evil, we must maintain ethical monotheism in the world at all costs.

With this understanding, we can begin to see why even children who generally are not biblically obligated to perform commandments until they are at least twelve (in the case of young women) and thirteen (in the case of young men) are included in this command to sanctify God's name. The Crusaders, as well as the Nazis, used children for their heinous crimes – and many religious Jewish leaders urged these children to die rather than to submit.

On what basis? Rabbi Yaakov Kaminetzky *z"tl*, a great Torah leader of our generation, makes the point in his biblical commentary *Emet L'Yaakov*, that the word "I must be sanctified (*v'nikdashti*)" in our verse under consideration, is in the passive rather than the active voice (*kidashti*). He suggests that this unusual grammatical construction comes to teach us that the commandment to sanctify God's name applies even to those who are generally not actively enjoined to perform commandments. The evils of idolatry, immorality and murder may not be allowed to be perpetrated; even children may not participate in such desecrations.

When Maimonides codifies this commandment of sanctifying the name of God, he begins the section: "The entire house of Israel is obligated to sanctify the name of God..." (Laws of the Foundations of Torah 5:1). Introducing a commandment with the expression, "The entire house of Israel," is unusual for Maimonides. And when we remember that in the Psalms of Hallel we find the phrase, "...He will bless the house of Israel..., the small ones along with the older ones" (Ps. 115:12–13), Rabbi Yaakov Kaminetzky finds further proof that the intent of Maimonides was to include children as well as adults in this commandment of sanctifying God's name.

In an amazing irony of history, only one page of a scholarly manuscript written by Rabbi Moshe Haim of Piotrekov, a great Torah sage who perished in the Holocaust, managed to survive World War II. Rabbi Moshe Haim was the father of Rabbi Yisrael Meir Lau, a former Chief Rabbi of Israel, who was liberated from the Buchenwald concentration camp at the age of eight. On this page is to be found a religio-legal analysis proving that children are obligated in the commandment of sanctifying God's name – utilizing the same texts brought by Rabbi Yaakov Kaminetzky several decades later.

We cannot love God and the good without hating evil and struggling against the wicked. We cannot preserve God and godliness without being willing to commit our lives – and the lives of children – for God's sake.

The Truest Holiness Resides in Human Beings

> *And the Lord spoke to Moses, saying: "Speak to*
> *the children of Israel and say to them, the feasts*
> *of the Lord, which you shall proclaim to be holy*
> *gatherings, these are My feasts."*
>
> LEVITICUS 23:1–2

The biblical book of Leviticus is called the book of holiness because it is suffused with "varieties of holy experiences"; the supreme place of holiness – the holy Temple; the seminal events of holiness – our festivals; and the familial "tribe" set aside for holiness – the kohanim – priests.

The Hebrew word *kadosh*, holy, literally means separate and exalted, an "other" which relates to the most supreme "Other One." Rudolph Otto, in his work *The Idea of the Holy*, calls the holy the numinous, the *mysterium tremendum*; mind wrestles with language to discover a proper metaphor for exploring those aspects most related to the Holy

One, Blessed be He. Our Bible associates holiness with time and place: On certain occasions, God allows us to have a special rendezvous or meeting with Him, and the festivals, *moadim*, are the "dates" He makes with us to enjoy His fellowship; there are certain places in which we can best feel His Divine Presence, such as the synagogue and study hall, places of worship of His name and the study of His word, all pale reflections of our destroyed holy Temple.

I would like to suggest that beyond the holiness of space and time, there is also a third window from which to gaze upon holiness – the human being created in the image of God. This window reveals itself in a unique law concerning the high priest on Yom Kippur. The convergence of Yom Kippur – the holiest day of the year, with the Holy of Holies – the holiest place in the holy Temple, was undoubtedly the zenith of the entire year. But amazingly, the Mishna teaches that if on the way to perform the Temple service, the high priest comes upon a dead body and there is no one else to bury the corpse, then the commandment to bury the corpse falls upon the high priest.

To understand the ramifications of this law, all we have to do is turn to the opening of our portion where the Torah establishes that the kohen-priest, whose raison d'etre is holiness, is forbidden to be defiled by the dead. The only exceptions are the priest's seven closest relatives: all others fall into the category of defiling the priest. And yet here the law commands the high priest himself to defile himself for a stranger. Clearly, the sanctity of the human body, even after its soul has departed (and all the more so for a living human being), transcends the sanctity of time and place.

In today's world, where many people walk out of the Sabbath's sanctity as easily as one steps out of a sukka, it's important to remember that one particular sanctity must bind us all, no less than the high priest is bound to the unburied stranger: appreciation and recognition of one's fellow human being created in the divine image as the essential ingredient of holiness. Not the mysterious Other, but the familiar Other. Holiness emanates from the fact that we are all inextricably bound to one another by the divine spark of the wholly Other which resides in each of us.

We can all learn an important lesson about the basics of human conduct – and respect for every human being – from the following story I heard from Mr. Mendel Reich, whose father's life in Auschwitz was saved by an extraordinary "coincidence." His father was scrupulous about the adage in *Ethics of The Fathers* to "…receive every person joyfully" (3:16), and made it a point to try to greet everyone warmly, and before they greeted him – no matter how young or strange the other person may have been.

The Polish town where his father lived was near the German border, and each morning on the way to prayers, he would meet a German nobleman out walking his dog. Every day, Mr. Reich would be the first to address his neighbor: "*A gutt morgen Herr Guttman, a gezunten tag.*" And Herr Guttman would nod condescendingly in return, barely mouthing or grunting a word spoken almost as a curse, "*Jude.*"

Years passed, and the elder Mr. Reich was sent to Auschwitz. One day, weakened from pneumonia, he found himself in the selection line, certain he would be sent to his death. Waiting, he said *vidui*, and the next moment he was standing in front of the Nazi guard who held his future destiny in his next word. Suddenly he recognized the German nobleman. "*A gutt morgen Herr Guttman, a gezunten tag,*" tremblingly whispered Mr. Reich. The Nazi guard looked at the Jew, and a flicker of recognition crossed his eyes. "*Jude,*" he whispered with his slight nod. "*Rechts!*" he called out. And Mr. Reich lived.

Israel – The State, Jerusalem – The City of Peace and Lovingkindness

> *And you shall count for yourselves from the morrow of the Sabbath [the first day of the festival of matzot], from the day in which you bring the* omer *offering lifted high, seven complete weeks shall there be.*
>
> LEVITICUS 23:15

What is the main function of the Jewish State, the State of Israel, and is that function substantively different from the significance of the City of Jerusalem and the holy Temple? Rabbi Avraham Yitzchak Hakohen Kook often made the point that the barley *omer* offering on the second day of the festival of matzot (Passover) permitted the new crop of grain to be eaten within the Land of Israel, and the two loaves of wheat bread that were brought on Shavuot seven weeks later permitted the new crop of grain for the holy Temple and Jerusalem. The two separate offerings and the daily counting between them emphasize both the difference as well as the connection between both concepts. What do these two places and ideals really signify and symbolize?

In order to understand fully, let me remind you of the momentous events which occurred during the First Commonwealth reign of King Hezekiah (seventh century BCE), a religious reformer who destroyed idolatry and restored the holy Temple to its proper place of glory. When Sennacherib, the King of Assyria, sent a great army to the ramparts of Jerusalem, "on that very night an angel of the Lord went out and struck down 185,000 people of the Assyrian camp" – enabling Hezekiah King of Judah to vanquish his powerful foe.

Unfortunately, neither Hezekiah's religious reforms nor his miraculous military victory bore the kind of positive fruit that might have emerged. In the words of the Talmudic sages:

> The Holy One Blessed be He desired to make Hezekiah the Messiah and Sennacherib Gog and Magog. Said the Measure of Judgment before the Holy One Blessed be He, "Master of the Universe, if You didn't make David King of Israel the Messiah after he praised You with so many songs and blessings [the book of Psalms!], how can You make Hezekiah the Messiah when, after You did all these miracles for him, he did not even praise You with one song?"
>
> *Sanhedrin* 94a

Imagine what Jewish history would have been like if only Hezekiah had given proper praise to God!

Wherein lay Hezekiah's fatal flaw? After all, the Talmud waxes poetic about the situation in Judah during his reign:

> Hezekiah planted a sword at the entrance to every House of Study, declaring that anyone who did not study Torah would be pierced by that sword. They later investigated and found that from Dan to Be'er Sheva there was not one ignorant Jew, that from Gvat to Antipatris there was not one male or female child,

not one man or woman, who was not completely conversant in the laws of ritual purity…

Sanhedrin, ibid.

So if everything was so good, why didn't Hezekiah give praises to God? The truth is that everything was not so good. After this outstanding military victory, the Bible reports:

> But Hezekiah did not reciprocate the benevolence that he was shown, for his heart became haughty… Hezekiah had very much riches and honor. He *made himself* treasure houses for silver, gold, precious stones… storehouses for produce of grain, wine and oil, and stables for… animals and herds. He made himself cities….
>
> II Chronicles 32:25–29

To make matters worse, when emissaries came from Babylonia "to inquire about the miracle that had occurred (outside Jerusalem)" (Ibid. 32:31),

> …Hezekiah showed them his whole treasure house – the silver, the gold, the spices, the fine oil, his warehouse and everything that was found in his treasuries; there was nothing that Hezekiah did not show them in his palace and in all his realm.
>
> II Kings 20:13

The prophet Isaiah even rebukes him for his crass conduct, telling him that all of his treasures, as well as some of his children, will be carted off to Babylonian exile (Ibid. 17, 18).

Hezekiah's fatal flaw stems from the fact that despite his desire to serve God and destroy idolatry, he remained enamored of all the trappings of a secular monarchy, especially the power and the wealth. Undoubtedly the very first concern of every state, including a Jewish state, must be to provide protection and sustenance for its citizens. The Torah understands this, and praises the Land of Israel for providing sufficient fruits and for serving as a safe fortress (the covenant with

Abraham, including boundaries) for the children of Israel. But the soul of the land must be Jerusalem and the holy Temple, the realization that all of our bounty comes from God and must be shared with the priests and the Levites, the widow and the orphan, the stranger and the unfortunate. This is the content of the speech-song made by the pilgrim Israelite when he brings his fruit, fruits of wheaten bread, to Jerusalem on Shavuot: "You shall sing and you shall say" – in the most correct translation) (Deut. 26:5–13). This is the connection between the *omer* sacrifice which address our gratitude for land, sustenance and protection; and the two loaves which addresses our profound gratitude to God and our spiritual sensitivity to the need to share with those who do not have, the message of the holy Temple. Once we show the world our holiness as a people, and our ability to forge a nation-state on the foundation stones of morality and compassion, the gentile nations will flock to our Temple to learn and accept a God and a world of truth and peace.

On Passover we left Egypt and became a nation because of the example of our power (the ten plagues, the Reed Sea); on Shavuot, we received in the Ten Commandments the model of our need to inspire the world by the power of our example, a holy nation, and therefore a kingdom of priest teachers to the world.

Hezekiah never really made this critical distinction, nor the necessary connection between the festival of matzot and the festival of Shavuot, between the barley *omer* offering and the wheat first-fruits offering, between the new crops for the land-state and the new crops for the Jerusalem Temple. He got stuck on the wealth and power of the state – and the prophet during his reign, Isaiah, describes a Jerusalem fraught with ritual religiosity but devoid of ethical sensitivity. He even forces people, indeed children, to study Torah by planting a sword in front of the Study Houses, and when Babylonian emissaries wish to understand the nature of the divine miracle, he can only point to his material wealth and power. Hezekiah lacks the song of the first fruits, the song which truly links him to God because it links him to all of the unfortunates, to morality and to compassion.

May we in reborn Israel make certain not to repeat Hezekiah's mistake and to sing the song of God and human concern when we sing our songs of praise on Israeli Independence Day!

The Passover Jew: The Beginning of a March as a Family Member

> *And you shall count for yourselves from the morrow of the Sabbath [the first day of the festival of Matzot] ... seven Sabbaths ... and you shall offer a new meal offering to the Lord.*
>
> LEVITICUS 23:15–16

Judaism teaches that all Israelites are responsible for each other, a co-signer for one's fellow Jew. Aside from the State of Israel – where the Jewish population has grown from six hundred thousand in 1948 to five and a half million today – the Jews in the rest of the world suffer from internal hemorrhaging, with the six million identifying American Jews in 1940 quickly moving toward halving itself by the end of the twenty-first century. So how do we "instruct" our errant Jewish siblings to remain within – or return to – Jewish peoplehood?

I believe that the very nature of the Hebrew calendar contains the direction toward the solution. Each year after the start of the Passover festival, we count each day toward the festival of Shavuot, a count which begins with our freedom from Egypt and culminates with the revelation at Sinai. The Hebrew term for the counting is *sefira*, a word pregnant with meaning, whose root verb, *s-p-r*, certainly is reminiscent of *sippur yetziat mitzrayim*, the retelling of the exodus from Egypt on the first night of the festival of matzot, and whose root noun is the Hebrew *sappir* (*samekh, peh, raish*), the dazzling blue-white sapphire diamond, its ethereal hues the colors of the heavens, bound up with the revelation. Immediately following the electrifying and inspiring revelation at Sinai, the Bible records:

> Moses and Aaron, Nadav and Avihu, and the seventy elders of Israel then went up. And they saw the God of Israel, beneath whose "feet" was something akin to the creation of a sapphire stone, like the essence of the heavens as to its purity.
>
> Exodus 24:9, 10

From this perspective, the days of our counting must be seen as a period of spiritual growth and development, demonstrating a linguistic and conceptual connection between Passover and Shavuot. Where and how does this spiritual journey begin? It begins with Passover, the first real encounter that God has with His nation Israel and its very conception. Our *sefira* count begins with a *sippur*, a tale, a story, a re-counting; the very essence of the Passover *seder* evening experience:

> And you shall tell [*haggada*, telling a story] your child on that day saying … (Ex. 13:8); "And Moses recounted (*vayesaper*) to his father-in-law all that the Lord had done to Pharaoh and to Egypt because of the Israelites …." (Ex. 18:8); "It is a positive commandment of the Bible to recount (*l'saper*) the miracles and wonders which were done to our forefathers in Egypt"
>
> *Mishneh Torah*, Laws of Ḥametz and Matza 7:1.

We must remember that the Israelites came into Egypt as a family, the seventy descendants of our grandfather Jacob-Israel. Hence, the recounting of the story of our enslavement and eventual redemption is iterated and reiterated by parents to their children as a familial recounting of family history because the Jewish nation is essentially an extended family. And, as in any family, there are familial memories of origins, of beginnings; in a family, there will always be a commonality, a togetherness that results from the good that flows through the veins of the family members. In a family there are special foods and customs, special holidays and celebrations; in a family there are mandated values and ideals, that which is acceptable and that which is unacceptable "in our family," and in a family there is a heightened sense of a shared fate and shared destiny, "all for one and one for all."

Family members willingly sacrifice for each other, helping each other monetarily, and in situations of life and death, even going so far as to donate a needed organ such as a kidney to keep a close relative alive.

Passover is our familial, communal festival, at the very beginning of our calendar, at the very outset of our unique history, at the early steps toward our *sefira* march, celebrated even before we received our Torah from God and before we entered the Promised Land. God, Torah, Land of Israel, Jerusalem, holy Temple had to wait for Shavuot. The Passover Sacrifice (Ex. 12), the source for our Passover *seder*, represents the celebration of our being part of a special, historic family even before we became a religion at Sinai. It emphasizes our willingness to sacrifice the lamb, a defiant act of rebellion against the bull-god of Egyptian slave-society, an act that attests to our uncompromising belief in human freedom and redemption – a belief that arose from the familial history of the pain of our enslavement and the murder of our children in the Nile River. Hence freedom for every individual became a familial passion for us and even an obsession.

In order to feel truly free, every person must feel that he/she counts (*sefira*); but that is how it is in families, where each member is called by his/her personal name and is known by his/her unique traits (both positively and negatively). It is for this reason that our Passover sacrificial meal must be subdivided into smaller – and more manageable – familial and extra-familial units, "a lamb for each household" or several households together. Special foods, special stories and special songs define and punctuate the familial nature of the event.

And the only ticket of admission is that you consider yourself a member of the family and wish to be counted in; this alone entitles you to an unconditional embrace of love and acceptance, to inclusion in the family of Israel. Theological beliefs and practices of religious observance are irrelevant; the only *rasha* (wicked son) is the one who himself excludes himself from the family – and even he/she is to be invited and sought after!

One of the rousing songs of the earlier part of the *seder* is *Dayenu*, ("It would have been enough"). "Had God only taken us out of Egypt, it would have been enough; had God merely brought us to Sinai and not given us the Torah, it would have been enough." Our sages teach that when the Israelites stood at Sinai they were one people with one heart, a united and communal family. The song *Dayenu* teaches that even a Jew who feels only a sense of familial oneness – even without the 613 commandments – would be extremely positive if not sufficient in itself.

How can we engage our Jews so that they do not defect and fall away from us? We must embrace them as part of our family, love them because we are part of them and they are part of us, regale them with the stories, songs and special foods which are expressed in our biblical national literature and which emerged from our fate and our unique destiny, share with them our vision and dreams of human freedom and peace, and accept them wholeheartedly no matter what. For some of them it may be the first step on their march to Torah and the Land of Israel on Shavuot; for others, it might be all they are interested in. And that too must be considered good enough, *Dayenu*! After all, the very first covenant God made with Abraham was the covenant of family and nation.

A Personal Family Postscript

My paternal grandfather was an idealistic and intellectual communist who wrote a weekly column for the Yiddish communist newspaper, *Freiheit*. On his kitchen wall were two pictures, one of Franklin Delano Roosevelt and the other of Joseph Stalin. He ate on Yom Kippur and truly believed that religion "was the opiate of the masses." Nevertheless, he conducted a Passover *seder* each year – which I attended as a young child – with matza, maror, haroset, and after the first part of the Haggada, he would add passages from the Prophets, the Talmud and Shalom Aleichem that dealt with consideration for the poor and underprivileged. Later he would check to make sure I could space my fingers properly for the Priestly Benediction, cautioning me to understand that the blessing was for world peace.

Despite my tender years, I noticed that there was still bread and rolls in the house, and if the visiting grandchildren wanted bread all they had to do was ask for it. I could not understand the contradiction (although I know now that *Pesaḥ Sheni*, exactly one month after the first *Pesaḥ*, provides a "second chance" for those who missed the regular Passover either because they were ritually impure, or "far away" physically or perhaps even religiously; since the Passover Meal at this *Pesaḥ Sheni* could be eaten even while there was *ḥametz* in the house, this ritual seems to have been strikingly similar to my grandfather's *seder!*) However, I could not understand why my grandfather bothered with a *seder* at all and why he was so proud of our being *kohanim* if he felt so far removed from the Jewish religion.

One day I was riding on a subway with my grandfather, and nearby sat two elderly ultra-Orthodox Jews, speaking in Yiddish. Two young toughs walked into our compartment and began taunting the hassidim. At the next stop my grandfather – who was fairly tall and strong – lunged forward, grabbed the toughs, and literally threw them out the open door. When he returned to his seat next to me, I asked, "But Grandpa, you're not at all religious." He looked at me in dismay. "What difference does it make? They are part of our family – and I am part of their family!" Then, I understood.

The Shavuot Jew

> And you shall count for yourselves from the
> morrow of the Sabbath [the first day of the
> festival of matzot] ... seven Sabbaths ... and you
> shall bring first fruits for the Lord.
>
> LEVITICUS 23:15–16

I s the Shavuot Jew superior to the Passover Jew? I have written about the count (*sefira*) of forty-nine days between Passover and Shavuot, days of Ḥol HaMoed (similar to the intermediate days of a festival) which expresses the connection between Passover – the very beginning of our inception as a nation, even before we received the 613 commandments of our Bible and even before we entered the Promised Land of Israel – and Shavuot, our end-goal, the day on which we received the Torah as well as the day we celebrate the festival of first fruits, which are brought to the holy Temple in Jerusalem.

From this perspective, the Passover Jew reflects God's covenant with Abraham (in Genesis); he feels first and foremost a profound familial connection with every Jew, a blood-bond which impels him to share in the Jewish fate – even if it means sacrificing his life – and to participate in the Jewish destiny. He connects with the familial stories of the origins of the family-nation of Israel, enjoys the special familial foods and major occasions of familial celebration or mourning (Passover matza, for example), and feels he is an integral part of the Jewish community.

The Shavuot Jew, on the other hand, relates to God's covenant with the nation of Israel at Mount Sinai, after the divine revelation of the Torah (Ex. 24:7–10). This Jew resides in Israel – after all, the festival celebrates the bringing of the first fruits to the Jerusalem Temple – and apparently accepts all of the commandments as attested to by the national proclamation preceding this second covenant, "we shall perform [the divine commands] and we shall internalize [or understand] them." The major motivation for the Passover Jew is his horizontal relationship with the Jewish peoplehood, the major motivation for the Shavuot Jew is his vertical relationship with God, his commitment to a higher law which it is his duty to observe.

There is yet one more aspect to the Shavuot Jew which must be emphasized: his vertical relationship to God ought to impel him to establish a profound horizontal relationship not only with his/her sibling Jews but also with every single human being on earth. If indeed God "created the human being in His image" (Gen. 1:27), each human being contains within him or herself a portion of that divine essence; if part of God is within me and part of God is within you, then we both share part of that same divine essence which binds each of us to the other in an inextricable bond. Our Bible commands:

> Observe the Sabbath day [a testimony of God's creation of all earthly creatures] to keep it holy…in order that your gentile male servant and your gentile female servant may rest like you."
> Deuteronomy 5:12, 14

Apparently this is because your gentile servant is essentially like you, endowed with that very same "image of God" which endows you with your ultimate and inviolate value.

This is precisely how Rabbi Abraham Ibn Ezra understands what is probably the most famous verse in the Bible:

"…You shall love your neighbor like yourself, I am the Lord" (Lev. 19:18). Says the Ibn Ezra, "One should love doing good to his friend as he would wish to do for himself, and the reason that this verse concludes with the words 'I am the Lord' is because 'I am the Lord' who has created you as one."

Ibn Ezra, ad loc.

Perhaps the most outstanding expression of this principle is the introduction to the daily prayer which was written by Rabbi Haim Vital and has been adopted by almost every prayer book of the Oriental Jewish communities:

Before one begins one's prayer, it is proper to say, "Behold, I accept upon myself the commandment of 'you shall love your neighbor like yourself.'"

Apparently, the very purpose of attempting to come close to the Almighty in prayer is so that we might come close to our fellow human beings created in the image of the one God. And this may very well be the deepest reason why we read the book of Ruth on Shavuot: the true Shavuot Jew feels the obligation to bring every human being, even a Moabite woman, under the wings of the Divine Presence, at the very least to accept the seven Noahide laws of morality (*Mishneh Torah*, Laws of Kings, 8:10) and maximally to accept the entire religion of Israel; after all, the prophets speak of all nations rushing to the Temple – a house of prayer for all people – from which will emanate the word of the Lord to the entire world (Isaiah 2; Micah 4). From what we have written thus far, it would certainly seem that the Shavuot Jew is far more complete – and praiseworthy – than the Passover Jew.

However, there is one particular flaw that often manifests itself in the Shavuot Jew, a danger and challenge that one must guard against: closeness to God not only often fails to enhance one's closeness to every Jew and every human being, but that very closeness to the divine sometimes serves to remove a person even further from a fellow Jew and fellow human being.

Rabbi Yaakov Yosef of Polonnoye suggests: "'With God did Noah walk' (Gen. 6:9); with God and not with humanity, so that Noah neither remonstrated with God on behalf of the world nor did he attempt to bring the errant children closer to their Father in heaven, as did Abraham."

Rabbi A.Y. HaKohen Kook, the first Chief Rabbi of Israel, says it very strongly:

> The soul of the sinners of Israel before the coming of the Messiah – those who are connected with love to all matters affecting the welfare of the Jewish people, the Land of Israel and its nation – is more perfected than the soul of the religious faithful of Israel who lack that fundamental feeling for the communal well-being and the renewal of the nation and the land.
>
> *Arpalei Tohar*, pp. 11–12

In other words, a Passover Jew who truly loves and sacrifices for his nation can sometimes be on a higher plane than the Shavuot Jew who is careful not to transgress God's commandments, but lacks true love for every Jew and the Jewish national mission. The Shavuot Jew often forgets his responsibility to the world, inspired by the portion of the universal God within each of us and confirmed by the divine charge to Abraham: "Through you shall be blessed all the families of the earth."

Postscript

The great Rabbi Yisrael Salanter would tell the following story, demonstrating how closeness to God can sometimes lead to creating distance from one's fellow Jew and fellow human being.

One day he was unexpectedly detained in Kovno, and he had to spend Yom Kippur there. When he entered the synagogue right before *Kol Nidrei*, the gabai, recognizing the important guest, immediately invited him to sit along the eastern wall, but Rav Yisrael preferred to stand in the back of the synagogue. At some point he noticed a man praying with great devotion, mouthing audibly the following prayer. "My Lord, before I was born I was not worthy, now that I have been born, it is as if I had never been born. I stand before You as a vessel filled with shame and humiliation."

As he mouthed these words tears were coursing down his cheeks. Rav Yisrael motioned to the gabai and asked to be seated in the empty seat next to that particular person. Rav Yisrael was much inspired by his seatmate, and this inspiration continued the following day until the end of the Torah reading. But when the gabai asked Rav Yisrael's seatmate to accept the honor of binding the Torah (*gelilah*), an entirely different personality seemed to emerge. When offered gelilah, the seatmate grew visibly angry, and began to fidget uncomfortably. "*Gelilah* is for fools," he muttered under his breath. "Give it to someone else." He looked as if he were about to suffer a veritable stroke! The great rabbi turned to his seatmate in confusion. "But did you not just weep over the fact that you are not worthy, that you are like a vessel filled with humiliation?"

"Yes, in comparison to the Almighty I am not worthy; but in comparison to these jokers and ignoramuses, who do not pray as fervently as I do, who do not spend as much time in the study of the Torah as I do, I certainly am worthy, much more worthy than they are!"

When the Sabbath Silences the Shofar

> *In the seventh month, on the first day of the*
> *month, shall be a solemn rest unto you, a day of*
> *the remembrance of the blast of rams' horns, a*
> *holy convocation.*
>
> LEVITICUS 23:23

The Torah portion of *Emor* deals with sanctity of place and person – via the kohanim-priests of the holy Temple, and sanctity of time, via a calendric description of the Shabbat and festivals. Let us look in depth at Rosh Hashana when it coincides with the Sabbath – and we will hopefully achieve more profound insight into the distinctive qualities of the festival and the Sabbath. The only commandment unique to Rosh Hashana is the blowing of the shofar. The shofar not only symbolizes the heart of Rosh Hashana, it has virtually entered the psyche of the Jewish nation as the instrument unique to us as a people. Although heard less often than the cry of the muezzin or the peal of church bells, the shofar's haunting sound reverberates for us in ways that seem to transcend time.

In its wail, we hear the travail of Jewish history, and in its triumphant clarion call, we see the dream of Jewish and world redemption.

The Talmudic sages (*Rosh Hashana* 33b) describe the staccato sound of the shofar as *ginuḥei ganaḥ* (the sighing sound of the thrice-heard *shevarim*), and *yilalei yalil* (the wailing sound of the nine times-heard *trua*); the strong, firm sound of the *tekiya* represents a shout of joy, praise and hope for the future – "*halleluhu b'teika shofar*" "praise Him with the blowing of the shofar" (Ps. 150:3). This combination of Jewish tears and Jewish faith is the quintessence of Judaism. For many whose presence inside a synagogue is limited to the High Holy Days, the shofar is the very essence of Judaism.

Nevertheless, when Rosh Hashana falls on the Sabbath day, despite the explicit commandment in the Torah to sound the shofar, the commandment is suspended. The Mishna deals with this apparently paradoxical law:

> When Rosh Hashana falls on a Sabbath, the shofar may be blown in the holy Temple, but not in the rest of the land....
>
> Mishna *Rosh Hashana* 4:1

Two reasons are given for this strange phenomenon (*Rosh Hashana* 29b). The most popularly cited is that we suspend the command to blow the shofar when Rosh Hashana falls out on the Sabbath, "lest one may come to carry the shofar..."

One doesn't have to be a skeptic to wonder why the sages would enact a decree which would remove the very soul of Rosh Hashana – its living, breathing symbol – and suspend the performance of one of the 613 commandments just because of the possibility that someone might pick that particular day for his shofar instruction, and thereby carry the shofar four cubits in the public domain or take the shofar from a private to a public domain.

Before we can understand the motivation behind this decree, we must first grasp why the act of carrying violates the sanctity of the Sabbath in the first place, especially since carrying doesn't seem to effectuate any of the constructive changes we associate with what is forbidden on the Sabbath. For example, it is easy to understand why lighting a fire, cooking a meal, painting a wall or writing a letter are considered creative physical activities, forbidden on the day dedicated to our realization that the Almighty is the only real and absolute Creator – not us. But how does carrying an object from one place to another in any way compromise the sole creatorship of God and the universal "creaturekind" of humanity?

I believe that the answer lies in the fact that Jewish law mandates transference of ownership by the removal of the object by its new owner from one domain to another; carrying an object from the home of the former owner to the outside public area constitutes an act of acquisition. It is fascinating to note, therefore, that paying in cash for a book, inside Steimatzky's for example, does not make one its owner; carrying the book outside on the other hand, does. With this understanding, the prohibition on the Sabbath against carrying an object from domain to domain, or four cubits in the public domain, becomes indubitably clear.

On the Sabbath, I am asked to remember that God created the world, the corollary of this truth being that everything in it belongs to Him, and not to me. By not carrying, I express in a real way that my property – even a handkerchief in my back pocket – also belongs to God.

Similarly, Rosh Hashana's essential message is the kingship of God over the entire creation. On this day, all ideas of property, possession and self-importance must be placed into proper perspective. The shofar announces the anniversary of the birth of the world. Whatever we are, whatever we possess, all of it and all of us belong to God, and only God.

Now when Rosh Hashana – which is a festival falling under the biblical rubric of "you shall rejoice in your festivals" – falls on a weekday, we are allowed to carry objects from domain to domain. As Maimonides explains, if we were prohibited from carrying it would compromise our ability to truly rejoice; it would be as though our very hands were being prohibited from our use. But when the Sabbath and Rosh Hashana coincide, both occasions owing their unique character to the expression of God's kingship and creatorship, the message is all the more powerful. When I refrain from so much as lifting the shofar on the Sabbath lest I carry it, I am bearing powerful testimony to God, sole King and Creator. The sages declare that the silence of the shofar on the Sabbath is an even more eloquent expression of God's kingship than would be the shofar's powerful blast.

There is a second reason for not blowing the shofar on Sabbath linked even more directly to this Torah portion, which refers to Rosh Hashana not only as the day of the shofar blast but this time as the "day of the remembrance of the shofar blast." When Rosh Hashana falls on the Sabbath, we only "remember" what the shofar blast sounds like, but we do not blast the shofar. Why not?

The answer lies in mystical perspective that sees the Sabbath as a marriage between God and the Jewish people. Indeed, the *Zohar* divides the Sabbath into three stages. Friday night is the engagement between God and Israel, with the *Lekha Dodi* prayer seeing Israel as husband, and *Shekhina* as beloved bride. This is followed the next morning by our thanksgiving for the Torah, the great wedding present which the Almighty gave to His people at Sinai. Finally, during the afternoon prayer, we speak of the *yiḥud*, the union, between God and Israel which consummates and climaxes the wedding ceremony.

If the Sabbath is a marriage, then festivals function as the engagement. The understanding of this symbolism raises a number of liturgical questions. We recite the *sheheheyanu*, praising the Almighty for granting us the well-being to reach this day, before each festival, but not before the advent of the Sabbath. Why not?

Furthermore, only when the festivals fall on the Sabbath do we insert the word "*be'ahava*" (with love) in the additional *Mussaf* prayer, specifically in praise of the Sabbath; on an ordinary festival, there is not this additional word of love. Why not?

Rabbi David Abudarham, in his commentary on the order of our prayers, explains that we only recite the *sheheheyanu* blessing on occasions which occur less frequently than every thirty days; such occasions are considered rare, and they therefore engender excitement and anticipation. This is not the case with the Sabbath, which falls each week.

The parallel should now be clear. Festivals are reminiscent of the special meetings between Israel and God, those rare occasions when we felt his presence in history; similar to the meetings between an engaged couple, which are often limited because of time and geographical constraints. Each meeting is anxiously anticipated – and the ardent suitor often brings a gift to his fiancée when they see each other.

The Sabbath relationship is more akin to that of a married couple, who are used to each other's presence and whose meetings together rarely inspire a rise in blood pressure (unless they are arguing, God forbid) or a special gift. However, the love between the married couple is far deeper than the feelings of an engaged couple; my wife is as inextricable a part of me as I am an inextricable part of her. "*Ishto kegufo,*" we are truly one organism, one existential being, whose shared bed, shared experiences and shared children make us indelibly bound to each other.

The excitement of the festival relationship inspires the *sheheyanu* blessing and the special gifts we bring to our heavenly "groom": the four species on Sukkot, the shofar on Rosh Hashana. The closeness of the Sabbath relationship – toward which we prepare all week – obviates the necessity of both *sheheheyanu* and the special gift of the shofar.

Engaged couples often need visible proof of their love, hence the constant purchase of gifts. But when a marriage is strong and solid, gifts are not necessary for proving one's love; the relationship speaks for itself.

The shofar on Rosh Hashana is a gift we bring to God. But the depths of our love for the Sabbath cannot be defined by a gift, no matter how rare and wonderful. Our love on the Sabbath is wordless, soundless, because it is ourselves that we give to God, in consummate love.

The shofar's silent testimony is pure. This is one time when less is more.

Behar

Israel Is Married to Its Land

*God spoke to Moses at Mount Sinai, telling him to
speak to the Israelites and say to them: When you
come to the land that I am giving you, the land
must be given a rest period, a sabbath to God. For
six years you shall plant your fields, prune your
vineyards, and harvest your crops, but the seventh
year is a sabbath of sabbaths for the land…*

LEVITICUS 25:1–5

The Torah portion of *Behar* opens with the fundamental laws
of *Shmitah*, the manifestation of God's total involvement in the land.
During these days when the issue of land is the ultimate question on
everyone's mind – for what is the issue of peace and war if not land – we
have to remind ourselves how it was possible that despite almost two
thousand years of exile, the Jews never stopped dreaming of their return
to the Land of Israel – and have indeed returned in our generation. Was
it something miraculous and mystical that sustained this relationship

of a people to land for so long? And if it was, wherein lies the origin of this unique relationship?

Ordinarily, Jewish law divides along two lines: requirements between human beings and God, and requirements between one human being and another. But there is also a third realm: the requirements of a Jew toward his/her land. In fact, the very climax of the book of Leviticus emphasizes precisely this third realm, *bein yehudi l'artzo*, between the Jew and his land, replete with laws of the tithing of produce, the necessity of allowing the land to lie fallow during the Sabbatical year, and returning all property to its original owner in the jubilee year.

But in order to grasp the full symbolism of a Jew's relationship to a land, and how this land is at the crux of our experience as Jews, we must take note of a much earlier biblical incident at the very dawn of our history, when our first patriarch purchased a plot for his wife's grave-site, paying an astonishingly high sum for a relatively tiny piece of land.

Abraham's purchase of this property not only provides us with biblical evidence that our deed to Hebron reaches back to our earliest beginnings; it unites our history with a specific parcel of earth, inextricably linking the founders of our faith-nation with the land of Israel in an eternal bond, within the boundaries of God's initial covenant with Abraham.

This purchase of land indelibly establishes for us the commitment which the Bible expects a husband and wife to have for each other, a commitment which extends beyond physical life and translates into a significant monetary expenditure. The sages of the Talmud derive our form of religio-legal obligatory engagement, *kiddushin* (with a ring or an object of material value), from Abraham's purchase of the plot of land that would serve as Sarah's cemetery plot (*Kiddushin* 2a). The Talmud deduces the "taking" of marriage from the "taking" of the land. Thus, halakha creates a metaphoric parallel between marriage, land and eternity, alluding to the unique and magnificent ideal that we must develop an eternal relationship of love and commitment to our land paralleling the eternal relationship of love and commitment to our spouse.

In order to understand what it means to be "engaged or married" to the land, let's first isolate three elements of marriage, and then trace these elements back to our portion of *Behar*. First of all, marriage contains the physical or sexual component, called "entrance" (*biah* in Hebrew), which expresses the exclusivity of the love relationship. Second, there are the fundamental obligations the couple has to one another, specifically outlined in the Bible (Ex. 21:10) and clearly delineated in the fifth chapter of the tractate *Ketubot*. Third, the Torah essentially sees marriage as an eternal relationship. Abraham's obligations to Sarah continue even beyond her lifetime, as we have seen, and the prophet Hosea describes God's engagement to Israel: "I shall consecrate you unto Me forever" (Hosea 2:21). Although divorce is an allowable option if there is no better solution, the rabbinic view at the conclusion of the Tractate *Gittin* remains operative: "Even the altar of the holy Temple weeps when a husband and wife are divorced" (*Gittin* 90b).

Undoubtedly, the ideal is the eternal relationship, and even when psychologies collide, biology heals: For the birth of a child, and the eternal potential of this new creature continuing after the death of each spouse, soon asserts the true continuity of the marital relationship.

We find that these three elements relate to the land of Israel as well! "When you come into the land," utilizes the the verb whose very root refers to sexual relations specific to husband and wife (*biyah*). And when we're told to hallow the fiftieth year (Lev. 25:10), the word the Torah employs is '*kiddashtem*' – the same term which is the rabbinic expression for marriage. The Torah parchment unfurled in *Behar* seems to weave a mystical marital canopy uniting the nation Israel with the land of Israel.

Second, no sooner have we entered the land than the Torah instructs us concerning our obligation to that land (much like the obligations a husband has to a wife): for six years we are obligated to plant the fields, prune the vineyards, and harvest the crops, "but the seventh year is a sabbath of sabbaths for the land…you may not plant your fields, nor prune your vineyards…since it is a year of rest for the land" (Lev. 25:4–5). The land must lie fallow every seventh year when its produce belongs to the poor who eat freely from the crops. And, in a veritably uncanny, human fashion, resembling the husband-wife relationship, the land responds to our actions, or our lack thereof. If we maintain our obligation to the land, the land will respond to us with abundant produce. If not, the land will grow desolate, for "as long as the land is desolate it will enjoy the sabbatical rest that you would not give it when you lived there" (Lev. 26:35). In other words, the land will lie fallow and unproductive. Hence, a relationship of mutuality exists between Israel and its land.

Third, just as there is an eternal aspect to marriage, there is also an eternal aspect to the land. During the jubilee, the fiftieth year, the Torah commands that land one was forced to sell returns to the original owners (Lev. 25:13). This is called redemption of property (*geulat karka*). Land remains in the family for perpetuity even when dire circumstances force a sale. The eternal link between the land and its owners is the issue addressed in the *haftara* of *Behar* when Jeremiah, the prophet of the destruction of the holy Temple, redeems his uncle Hananel's land for him. Despite the destruction at hand, Jeremiah knows that eventually the Jews will return to the land. God's promise of an eternal covenant is paralleled in the eternal rights of a family toward its property.

Throughout the world, people love the land in which they are born, a love so central that one's homeland is called in most vernaculars "motherland" or "fatherland." These terms are absent in the Hebrew language; our relationship to the land is not one of son or daughter to father or mother, but is rather akin to that of husband to wife or wife to husband. May we be worthy of the land and may the land properly respond to our love and commitment to it in this generation of return and redemption.

Count toward Purity

> *You shall count for yourself seven cycles of*
> *sabbatical years, seven years, seven times; the*
> *years of the seven cycles of sabbatical years shall*
> *be for you forty-nine years.*
>
> LEVITICUS 25:8

The biblical portions in the book of Leviticus – *Tazria, Metzora, Emor* and *Behar* – seem to be almost fixated on the commandment to count, the commandment of *sefira*. Barely two chapters ago we were commanded:

> And you shall count for yourselves – from the day following the
> rest day [the first day of the festival of Passover], from the day
> when you bring the *omer* of the waving – seven weeks…until the
> day after the seventh week you shall count fifty days.
>
> Leviticus 23:15–16

The Bible has commanded us to count each day of the seven weeks between the festivals of Passover and Shavuot, until the fiftieth day. And now in this portion of *Behar* the Bible is commanding us to count the seven cycles of the sabbatical years (seven times seven or forty-nine years) until the fiftieth year, the jubilee year. Clearly, there is a significant parallel between these two commandments of counting. In a similar way, both men and women (*zav* and *zavah* as well as *nidah*) are commanded to count seven days, after which – on the eighth day – they undergo ritual immersion and purity. All of these "countings" must in some way be related.

The count from Passover to Shavuot is – at least from a clear biblical perspective – the count from freedom from slavery into the desert to our entry into Israel and Jerusalem. Yes, on Passover we left Egypt and Egyptian enslavement; however, we only got as far as the desert, with all of the uncertainties of the desert and all of the alien and difficult climatic and agricultural conditions of the desert. It is specifically Shavuot which is biblically defined as the festival of the first fruits, which could be brought to the holy Temple in Jerusalem only once we arrived at the place of our inheritance (Lev. 23:17). The Bible underscores the relationship between Shavuot and Jerusalem when it discusses the special declaration to be made by the Israelite upon bringing the fruits to the Temple altar (Deut. 26:1, 2).

Passover is therefore our freedom from Egypt and slavery; Shavuot is our entry into Israel and Jerusalem, replete with the holy Temple. This idea is even further deepened by the text of the Haggada during the Passover *seder*. The Mishna (in *Arvei Pesaḥim*) teaches that the central part of our retelling of the exodus from Egypt is an explication of the very verses which the individual must read when he brings the first fruits; we are to explicate around the *seder* table "from '*Arami oved avi*' [An Aramean tried to destroy my forefather] until the end of that portion" (Deut. 26:5–10). However, we do not explicate the entire speech; the Haggada neglects to include the last two verses of the declaration of the one who brings the first fruits. The Haggada quotes:

> An Aramean tried to destroy my forefather; he descended to Egypt…became great, strong and numerous. The Egyptians… afflicted us…we cried out to the Lord our God who heard our

voice, saw our affliction, and took us out of Egypt with a strong hand…with signs and with wonders.

Deuteronomy 26:5–8

However, the final two verses, "He brought us to this place, and He gave us this land, a land flowing with milk and honey; and now behold I have bought the first fruit of the earth that you have given me, O Lord" (Ibid 26:9, 10), are deleted by the author of the Haggada.

I heard it said in the name of a great talmudic giant of the last century that the reason for this deletion is that our entry into the Land of Israel is only destination and not destiny. I would respectfully maintain that the very opposite is the case. Our sojourn in Egypt and even our escape from Egypt were very much directed by God and were part and parcel of Jewish fate. Our entry into Israel, our establishment of our holy Temple in Jerusalem and our ability to influence the world to accept a God of morality and peace through the teachings of the holy Temple are very much dependent upon our own desires and actions. It is the desert which was a temporary destination; Israel and Jerusalem are the Jewish destiny of being a light unto the nations of the world.

That is why the Bible commands, "And *you* shall sanctify the fiftieth year" within the context of our counting of the sabbatical years leading up to the jubilee. And the very word jubilee is either identified with the word for shofar or ram's horn – the instrument used as our call to repentance – or from the Hebrew *yovel* which means "he (the nation) shall lead" the entire world back to God. The very jubilee year is biblically defined as a declaration of universal freedom and the return of every individual to his homestead, obvious expressions of redemption.

This march of national freedom from Egyptian slavery to security in our own land from which we must realize our mission to bring peace to the world is expressed by counting, or *sefira*. The Hebrew *s-p-r* also means to tell, to recount, to clarify – which is the real commandment of the *seder* night of *sipur yetziat mitzrayim*. The same root *s-p-r* also appears in the biblical description of the throne of the divine at the time of the revelation at Sinai, which is like "the white of the sapphire (*sappir*) and the purity of the heavens" (Ex. 24:10). From this linguistic perspective, it becomes necessary to understand the commandment to count – *sefira* – as a commandment to become pure and to move closer to the throne of the Almighty. Since there is no redemption without repentance and purification, we now understand why Shavuot is also the time when we receive the Torah from God – our road map to purity and redemption – and why Shavuot is truly the festival of our destiny. We now also understand why mystical and Hassidic literature refers to the emanations of the divine in this world as *sefirot*.

Postscript: Lag Ba'Omer – The Mystery Holiday

One of the strangest and most puzzling of the festivals of the Jewish Calendar is Lag Ba'Omer, the thirty-third day of the counting of the *omer*, which brings in its wake a respite from the mourning period between Passover and Shavuot; wedding celebrations abound, and the heavens are ablaze all night with the bonfires for which the youngsters have been collecting wood since the conclusion of Passover. Rabbi Yosef Karo's *Code of Jewish Law* (mid-sixteenth century) comments that "we are accustomed to call the day, the celebration of Rabbi Shimon Bar Yohai"; in Israel an abundance of prayers are recited and candles lit at the site of his holy grave (Meron in the Galilee, not far from Safed), and it is said that "he departed [from the physical world] on that day and also that he left the cave on that day" (*Oraḥ Ḥayim* 493:7). Apparently the origin of the festival is shrouded in mystery, and the true reason for its having turned into a day of weddings and bonfires is not really known. Perhaps if we analyze the cave experience of Rabbi Shimon Bar Yohai as well as attempt to understand the uniqueness of his teaching, we may succeed in solving the riddle of the significance of Lag Ba'Omer.

A chilling historical episode is recorded in the Talmud:

> Rav Yehuda, Rav Yose and Rav Shimon Bar Yohai were sitting together and discussing the Roman Empire. Rav Yehuda declared, "How magnificent are the accomplishments of that nation. They established marketplaces, bridges and bathhouses." Rav Yose was

silent. Rav Shimon Bar Yohai was critical. "They established mar-ketplaces to make room for the prostitutes, bathhouses to spoil themselves with pleasures, and bridges in order to collect taxes and tolls." When the conversation was overheard and told to the Roman authorities, Rav Yehuda was rewarded for his praise with an official appointment, Rav Yose was castigated for his silence with exile to Zippori, and Rav Shimon was punished for his indictment with the death penalty hanging over his head as a consequence. The great sage escaped with his son to hide out in a cave, where they miraculously subsisted on carobs and water (a carob tree and a well miraculously sprang up to their aid), and devoted twelve years to the exclusive study of the secrets of the Torah. Upon being informed that the Caesar had died and the death decree had been canceled, father and son exited from the cave. They immediately encountered a Jewish farmer plowing and planting, and cried out in disbelief: "How can you forsake the eternal world and occupy yourself with momentary pursuits?" A blazing fire came forth from their eyes, and a voice came down from heaven, thundering "Did you leave the cave to destroy My world?" and they returned to the cave. At the conclusion of another year they left the cave again, this time, seeing an elderly Jew running late Friday afternoon with two myrtle twigs. Upon discovering that the twigs were meant to adorn his Sabbath table, one symbolizing the command to "Observe the Sabbath to keep it holy" and the other symbolizing the command to "Remember the Sabbath and keep it holy'" they were comforted in their re-entry into society.

Shabbat 33b

What new truth did Rabbi Shimon Bar Yohai learn from the elderly Jew at the time of his second exit from the cave? I would submit that the initial cave experience of total immersion in sanctity and Torah study merely served to intensify Rabbi Shimon's neo-platonic division of the world into the two divergent planes of the holy and the secular, the spiritual and the material, with his denigration of everything that was physical; hence his negative attitude toward Rome and his disgust at the agricultural pursuit of the farmer. Rabbi Shimon would certainly have championed a *"kollel"* way of life for one's entire life – cloistering oneself in the House of Study and shutting out the world at large – as the only sincere way to save the divine.

The elderly Jew taught Rabbi Shimon that the sanctity of the Sabbath is meant to express the possibility – and challenge – of endowing the secular with the imprint of the holy, of transforming the very physical matter into the higher form of the spirit; after all, is not a Sabbath meal replete with *zmirot*, words of Torah and family harmony, a truly religious experience, and does not the sanctity of the Sabbath demonstrate the necessity of the spiritual penetrating, refining and uplifting the physical? Indeed, Rabbi Kook taught that the world is not divided into two distinct realms – the holy and the secular – but rather it is divided into two fluid and ready-to-combine entities, each of which has its ultimate source in the divine: the holy and the not-yet-holy, the religious and the not-yet-religious.

We have been given two commands, to observe the Sabbath on the Sabbath day and to remember the Sabbath – or to prepare for the Sabbath – during the other days of the week. Insofar as the possibility exists of plowing and planting in order to produce myrtle twigs for the Sabbath table, as long as the experience of plowing takes into account the biblical prohibition against using an ox and an ass together (which will cause the animals undue effort and pain), as long as the act of planting includes the prohibition of setting into the ground diverse seeds which would pervert the proper structure and order of nature, and as long as the farmer sets aside a portion of his land to be worked on by the poor and gives proper tithes to those who have no means of earning a livelihood – then the very acts of planting and plowing become acts of spirituality.

I would submit that Lag Ba'Omer is the day when Rabbi Shimon Bar Yohai left the cave for the second time and encountered the old man running with the two myrtle twigs just before sundown on Friday. The message he learned is actually provided by the continuation of the Talmudic story:

> Rav Shimon Bar Yohai then said: "Since a miracle occurred (and I was saved from death at the hands of the Romans) I ought to

establish some kind of improvement..." [when our ancestor Jacob emerged whole from his encounter with Esau, the progenitor of Rome, the Bible informs us that he encamped at the face of the city (Gen. 33) which Rav interprets to mean that he minted coins for them (similar to tax money)], Shmuel interprets it to mean he established market places for them, and Rav Yohanan interpreted it to mean he established bathhouses for them.

Shabbat 33b, 34a

Ultimately, the Gemara concludes that he purified a parcel of land which others had treated as ritually impure. Clearly, Rabbi Shimon Bar Yohai suddenly realizes that the societal materialistic improvements established by Rome were not evil in themselves; indeed, they were the very same improvements effectuated earlier by our forefather Jacob. Every aspect of the material world can potentially be sanctified, depending upon how it is used. And one's greatest task in this world is purifying an area which had hitherto been considered to be defiled!

I do not believe that I am moving too far afield when I remind you that the myrtle twigs of the old man is the same myrtle which – in the form of a wreath – was the imperial symbol of Rome, worn as a crown by the victorious emperors. The Torah must find the way of sanctifying the world, of sanctifying Rome, of bringing our morality to the mightiest powers on earth. The area which is actually impure and waiting to be purified is Rome itself, symbolized by the myrtle twigs used in the service of the Sabbath, witness to the fact that the entire world must be claimed by the God who created it!

Finally, what Rabbi Shimon bar Yohai learned on that fateful and glorious Sabbath eve when he left the cave for the second time caused him to disagree with his arch-disputant Rabbi Yehuda concerning the interpretation of a biblical verse we usually read on the Sabbath immediately before Lag Ba'Omer: "If you will keep My statutes (and the millennium shall arrive) ... I shall cause wild beasts to cease from the land" (Lev. 26:6). Rav Yehuda understands this to mean that wild beasts will be removed from the land, whereas Rav Shimon interprets the words to teach that the wildness of the beasts will cease to be in existence (Sifra 2:1); and Rav Shimon uses as his proof text the Psalm, "A Song for the

Sabbath" (Ps. 92:1), the day when we attempt to sanctify every materialistic aspect of life, from wine to books to song.

I believe that the Sabbath has taught Rabbi Shimon that there is no absolute physicality, or even absolute evil, in this world; every object, thought or experience has the potential to be sanctified, to be endowed with the holy.

Sexual immorality can destroy the world, and marital sexual intimacy can join two individuals as one and create new life. Fire can destroy lives, and the kindling fire of Sabbath peace can point the way toward love, harmony and redemption. If indeed Lag Ba'Omer is the anniversary of Rabbi Shimon's second exit from the cave, can there be any better way of celebrating such a milestone and honoring the memory of such a great Jewish sage than by the celebration of weddings of sanctity (*kiddushin*) and bonfires of warmth, friendships and songs dedicated to Israel, Torah and God?

And is it not critical that during our count from Passover – redemption promised – to Shavuot – redemption realized – from the prohibition of any form of leavening to the bringing of two *ḥallot* into the holy Temple, from the commitment of the Paschal sacrifice to the revelation of the 613 Commandments, we mark Lag Ba'Omer, which teaches us that sanctity is derived not from the destruction of the material but rather from the uplifting (and redemption) of the material.

Jubilee: Salvation for the World

> *And you shall sanctify the fiftieth year... it shall be a jubilee...*
>
> LEVITICUS 25:10

Is the jubilee year an Israel concept or a world concept?

I believe the answer lies in a proper understanding of the portion of *Behar*, but requires an introduction from the very earliest verses of the Bible. Our "Book of Books" is universal in its scope, vision and ethos, opening as it does with the majestic words, "In the beginning, God created the heavens and the earth." The biblical reach goes far beyond Israel and the Jew; our God is God of the universe, and He has created the human being – not only Jew – in His own divine image.

Neither Adam nor Noah was ready to accept the divine morality of the freedom and the inviolability of the human being, or to subject themselves to the personal discipline and delayed gratification necessary for the structuring of a truly moral world. The delicious fruit and tantalizing wine of the moment were too tempting for each of them.

The Bible continues, and from the three sons of Noah – Shem,

Ham and Yafet – are derived the seventy nations of the world. They build a city and a tower whose top extends to the heavens in order to make for themselves a (grandiose) name; God confounds their materialistic and selfish goals by making "babble" of their speech so that they do not understand – and so cannot communicate with each other – and scatters them all over the face of the entire earth.

God then elects Abram, establishing a covenant with this first Jew, whereby He guarantees him progeny (which will never be destroyed) and the land of Israel (to which Israel will ultimately return). God makes Abram into an eternal nation.

However, God has not chosen Abram to the exclusion of the world. Much the opposite, God changes Abram's name to Abraham, from "exalted father" (*Av ram*) to "father of a multitude of nations" (*Av hamon goyim*) (Gen. 17:4, 5). Even before the name change, God charges Abraham with the divine mission that "through you shall be blessed all the families of the earth" (Gen. 12:3), since Abraham must found a "holy nation and kingdom of priest-teachers who will lead the world to morality, peace and redemption. Israel must become God's entrance-way into the world.

It should not come as a surprise to find that the Bible views Israel as a mirror of – and eventually a model for – the entire world; Israel is the heart, conscience and reflection of the world, as well as the means for the repair (*tikkun*) of the world. So if the three sons of Noah fathered the seventy nations of the world, it makes sense that the three patriarchs – Abraham, Isaac and Jacob – fathered the seventy souls who came down to Egypt and formed the Jewish nation (Ex. 1:5). Jacob's dream ladder is rooted in the earth with its "top extending to the heavens" (Gen. 28:12), and the Midrash on virtually all of the verses of this dream sequence identify the place of dreams as Mount Moriah, Jerusalem and the ladder as being the holy Temple, paralleling the ladder and the temple with the tower-ziggurat of Babel. When the Jews are not worthy, they too will be exiled and scattered to all four corners of the world, just as God scattered the babbling nations all over the face of the earth. Eventually the city of Jerusalem and the holy Temple-tower in its midst will serve as a *tikkun* (repair) for the Tower of Babel, when its Torah of peace will spread to the west, the east, the north and the south, when all nations rush to it and become united not for the sole reason of self-aggrandizement, but rather for the sake of service to God:

> Then shall I transform for the nations one clear speech for all of them to call on the name of the Lord, to serve Him shoulder to shoulder.
>
> Zefaniah 3:9

Nowhere is our function as a model for the world more clearly expressed than in the portion of *Behar*, where the land of Israel is set up to be worked for six years, granted a sabbatical (both the land and its owners) on the seventh, and when all debts are likewise to be rescinded. After the seventh sabbatical, the fiftieth year becomes the jubilee:

> And you shall sanctify the fiftieth year, and declare freedom for the land and all of its inhabitants; it shall be a jubilee for you, when every person shall return to his/her homestead, family and family estate….
>
> Leviticus 25:10

The jubilee reflects our national dream – and mission – for world redemption; "the land" in the verse just cited may well refer to the entire land which God created together with the heavens, and on which all of humanity must be free and secure.

The founding fathers of Israel – like David Ben-Gurion – may not have been observant Jews, they may not even have consciously believed in God, but they did believe in the necessity for the Jewish homeland, and they shared in the biblical vision of our mission to the world. They understood the necessity of the land of Israel for the future of the Jewish people and of the necessity of Israel's Ten Commandments for the future of the world. They were idealists, who were profoundly committed to an ideal greater than they were and were selfless in their pursuit of this ideal.

Even though the Agranat Commission did not find her responsible for the failures at the beginning of the Yom Kippur War, Golda Meir resigned nonetheless, deeply disappointed in herself because she

believed she had disappointed her nation. Israel for them – and for
the Bible – is Jewish past and Jewish future, but is also a reflection of
the world, a cosmos-in-miniature, whose origins and whose destiny is
inextricably bound up with a vision of unusual salvation in a jubilee of
peace and freedom for all.

Jubilee Is True Freedom

And you shall sanctify the fiftieth year, and declare freedom for the land and all of its inhabitants; it shall be a jubilee for you...

LEVITICUS 25:10

The very word "jubilee" has become synonymous with the number fifty – an anniversary of a couple's marriage as well as a major milestone in the independence of a nation. The Bible even goes one step further: every fiftieth year all Hebrew slaves were given their freedom and all lands reverted to their original owners. All of society was given a reprieve and an opportunity for a new beginning. After all, individuals sold themselves into slavery because they saw no other option for economic self-preservation, and they were sold into slavery by the courts if there was no other way for them to make restitution for goods they had stolen; in an agrarian society, people sold their homestead only when they saw no other way to put bread in their mouths. Hence, the jubilee year provided economic recovery and opportunity for every citizen of Israel.

But the Bible goes beyond an "Economic Recovery Act" when it declares that the essential task of the jubilee is "to give redemption (*geula*)" to the land as well as to the people who dwell on the land (Lev. 25:9–10, 24). Redemption is a super-charged term which resonates with echoes of utopia, millennium and messianism, the ultimate vision of peace, security and the pursuit of happiness for all of humanity. How does the jubilee year prepare us for the very goal which the Bible insists we shall eventually achieve?

To probe deeper in the nature of this 'jubilee' year, perhaps a linguistic investigation into the unique Hebrew word *yovel* (jubilee) will help us. Nahmanides suggests that the Hebrew *yovel* means to walk, lead or direct, on the basis of the declaration of "freedom" (Hebrew, *dror*) of the fiftieth year. After all, the first and most obvious expression of freedom is the ability to walk wherever one wishes to go, the right to lead the way and the confidence to direct one's own destiny. A slave is subject to his master's desire as to where and when he moves; a servant is an object rather than a subject, is led and cannot lead, is directed and dare not direct. *Yovel*, the individual who can dwell (*"dur"* from *dror*) wherever he wishes, who can lead himself to his desired dwelling place, is truly free.

Foreign domination, and especially subjugation and enslavement, are an objectification and perversion of human dignity and majesty. Our sages compare a pauper to one who is dead, because in the midst of a frantic search for fundamental subsistence, there is neither time nor energy to express the unique human qualities of intellect and creativity.

Hence, the jubilee year "proclaims liberty throughout the land and to all its inhabitants" first and foremost by enabling every individual the freedom to return to his ancestral homeland and by giving him the opportunity for a fresh economic start. On a national level, Maimonides emphasizes the fact that Hanukkah is a festival of praise to the Almighty if only for the fact that political independence was regained by Israel for two hundred years. Political and economic freedom is the first stage of redemption.

There is an alternative interpretation of *yovel* offered by Rashi (ad loc.), who defines *yovel* as referring to the sounding of the ram's horn. His source is a famous Talmudic discussion in which Rabbi Akiva declares, "When I went to Arabia, they used to call a ram a *yobla* (*Rosh Hashana* 26a)."

Then this jubilee "year of the ram's horn," as Rashi takes it, would evoke a more substantive form of redemption: Torah, the laws and statutes which govern Jewish life. When the Ten Commandments are about to be given on Mount Sinai, we read the prohibition against anyone actually touching the mountain, and only when "the ram's horn (*hayovel*) is sounded with a long blast, shall they come up to the mountain" (Ex. 19:13). Thus it's a ram's horn that paves the way for Torah, that is identified with the sound of the divine revelation (*kol*), and so in the Rosh Hashana liturgy it is *shofarot* or the sound of the ram's horn which is the call of return to the Torah.

What is a shofar? At Sinai, the shofar was intimately linked with the giving of the Torah. After all God commanded "…when the ram's horn [*hayovel*] ceased to be sounded, they (the people) may come up the mountain" (Ex. 19:13). This implies that as long as the shofar was heard, the Torah was still being revealed, and Mount Sinai was "out of bounds" for all but Moses; *yovel*-ram's horn is thereby identified with Torah, giving different word explanations for the same conceptual idea.

The freedom declared by the jubilee year grants the opportunity to the Jew to realize his true potential, to express his most fundamental essence grounded in the roots of his very being. Rashi insists that this truest essence of the Jew is Torah, the word of God symbolized by the sound of the ram's horn at the time of the revelation. Otherwise, how can we explain the amazing midrash that every fetus in its mother's womb is taught Torah by an angel of God? Our sages are hereby insisting that Torah is the most fundamental ingredient of the existential soul of every Jew! Our most basic identity, our vocation and avocation, our source and our purpose, is Torah – its theoretical teaching as well as the more perfect society it commands us to form.

The formula contains one additional equation. What are the specific commands effectuated during the jubilee year? Slaves go free, debts are rescinded, family homesteads are returned to their original owners; it is also a sabbatical year, so that the land as well as its owner rests from the physical labor of working the land. Every seventh year is parallel to every seventh day; instead of working his land, the farmer will hopefully work his mind in the vineyard of Torah, furrowing and planting spiritual ideas and ideals in the lanes of his brain.

Most individuals only realize a small percentage of their potential; most of us are "blocked" by all sorts of physical and psychological barriers. We cannot do what we really wish to do, what we are truly capable of achieving, either because a foreign government or a tyrannical employer does not allow us to, or because poverty and the pursuit of bread do not afford us the time and the energy to express ourselves properly ("at the expense of his soul-roots does he bring his bread" chants the cantor on Yom Kippur), or because negative and damaging early childhood experiences cripple our ability to be truly productive.

With this understanding, we can now ponder the genius of the jubilee year. Every Jew becomes free from external domination; returning to his own land under his own government; fruits and vegetables may be eaten freely without back-breaking labor; debts which enslave the poor to their creditors are rescinded; and a year of Torah study hopefully frees every Jew from the psychological limitations and addictions which imprison his soul-psyche. Freedom from a Jewish perspective doesn't mean that one is free to do nothing; freedom means that one has the unfettered ability to express one's truest self, to realize one's greatest potential. Freedom does not mean escape from responsibility for oneself and one's actions because of "toxic" parents or a negative social environment: much the opposite, freedom suggests the ability to assume responsibility for oneself and one's actions in the fullness of one's maturity. Such freedom enables us to return to our initial and primordial roots, to re-activate the "image of God" in which we were created and to bring the redemption by restoring the harmony of Eden before humanity fell.

True freedom is therefore connected to our initial and eternal humanity, to the spark of the divine within each of us, and our becoming what and who we are truly capable of becoming. From a biblical perspective, Torah is the means by which all of this can happen, because it is the Torah which can enable the individual to overcome his various blocks, to assume control of his instincts and destiny, and to transform and re-shape humanity and society into what it initially was at the dawn of Creation. No wonder the Mishna in *Avot* teaches: "No one can be considered free except those who occupy themselves in Torah" (6:2). Both Rashi and Nahmanides agree this is true freedom!

I would like to add another nuance to our understanding of the word *yovel* or jubilee. The portion of *Behar* and its theme of jubilee always falls during the period between Passover and Shavuot. Concerning *yovel*, the Torah states:

> And you shall count seven sabbaths of seven years, that is seven times seven years; the period of the seven sabbaths of years shall thus be forty-nine years.
>
> Leviticus 25:8

This serves as a striking parallel to the forty-nine days of counting between Passover, when we first mark our physical freedom from Egyptian slavery into the desert and progress toward the festival of Shavuot, which celebrates our bringing of the first fruits to the holy Temple in Jerusalem; Passover, when we experienced the God of Freedom (*ḥerut*), Shavuot, when we received the entire Torah at Mount Sinai seven weeks later (*aḥrayut*). We have seen how, according to Nahmanides, the word *yovel* means to walk, even to walk quickly, which has the image of a steady progression. This period from exodus to Sinai, form the beginnings of physical freedom to complete spiritual independence with Torah and holy Temple in Jersualem, constitutes a steady progression. This idea is preserved in the kabbalistic identification of each of the forty-nine days between Passover and Shavuot as a spiritual journey and a religious ladder upon which one must progress in order to receive the Torah and be worthy of complete redemption. In a similar manner must we view as a spiritual progression the count of forty-nine years, seven sabbaths of years between the first sabbatical year and the seventh, which climaxes in the jubilee year; our return to our ancestral homeland in the fullness of physical and spiritual freedom. With the jubilee year, we experience the intentions of our most profound, national good and universal vision, when the chains of slavery and economic deprivation are removed and a life dedicated to human values, economic opportunity and human rights for every person on the planet may finally be achieved.

The Land of Israel Is the Land of God

> *I am the Lord your God who brought you forth*
> *out of the land of Egypt to give you the land of*
> *Canaan to be your God.*
>
> LEVITICUS 25:38

One of the most thought-provoking statements in the Babylonian Talmud posits that only if one lives in the land of Israel does one have a God, while living outside the land of Israel is the equivalent of not having a God (*Ketubot* 110b). The proof text the sages turn to is the verse in the portion of *Behar* quoted above.

Rashi in his commentary quotes the Talmud in *Ketubot*, but with a slightly different formulation: "Whoever lives in the Land of Israel, I am God to him; whoever goes out of Israel is as one who serves idols." Here too, the text is equating the exile (or Diaspora) with idolatry, but the transgression of idolatry is specifically placed upon one who lived in Israel and left, rather than on one who was born in the Diaspora and remained there. Nevertheless, how are we to understand that to have or not to have a God depends on the stamp in your passport? Do people outside the land not also believe in God? Is God only to be found in Israel?

The Penei Yehoshua suggests the following interpretation: The Land of Israel is qualitatively different from any other land in the world in that what happens to the Israelites within it is a direct result of divine activity and intervention. Elsewhere the major influence comes from God's messengers, so to speak, such as the natural forces of sun, wind, rain and rivers, the stars of the zodiac, and the astrological movements of the heavens. In Israel, God Himself directs the destiny of its inhabitants. The Sochaczower Rebbe, Rabbi Abraham Bornsztain, takes this idea one step further and applies it to Jews of Israel accepting financial help from Diaspora communities. He writes:

> If a person lives in the land of Israel but his livelihood depends on the Diaspora, he is not a servant of God but a servant of His servant – the angel who governs the land from which his income is coming. Such a situation does not fulfill the obligation to inhabit the land, and this person may as well stay in the Diaspora. This is the reason many Torah scholars and leaders chose not to emigrate to the Land of Israel.
>
> Avnei Nezer on *Yoreh Deah*, 454

These interpretations, however, do not connect the unique relationship between God and the land of Israel into the major laws of this Torah portion – the Sabbatical and jubilee years. In this regard, Rabbi Shlomo Efraim Luntchitz, in his commentary *Kli Yakar*, provides the key. He initially explains the reason for which we are commanded to leave the lands of Israel fallow in the seventh (sabbatical) year as being necessary ecologically: in order to replenish the soil and strengthen it for further plantings, a suggestion made earlier by Maimonides. However, he is forced to reject this agricultural reason because, if that were indeed the reason behind the biblical commandment, the punishment for not keeping the sabbatical year should have been a crop failure during the eighth year due to an unnatural depletion of the soil, instead of the punishment of exile. If the reason why we do not work the land during the seventh year is in order to enrich our natural national and earthly resources, then the Torah should not have written, "a Sabbath unto God," but rather "a Sabbath unto the land" since the purpose was totally in terms of the soil being enriched by enforced rest.

The Kli Yakar then provides a reason close to the idea preferred by the Avnei Nezer, but he links it to the laws of the Sabbatical and jubilee years. The intelligent individual could imagine that after allowing the land to lie fallow during the Sabbatical year – and in the event of the jubilee, the land would lie fallow for two whole years – the Israelites would not have enough to eat during the following year. The fact that they did, demonstrated to them – as well as to the rest of the world – that Israel and her people were directly guided by the divine, and not by the usual laws of nature, climate and agriculture.

Rabbi Yitzhak Arama gives a further interpretation, seeing in the Sabbatical-jubilee cycle an allegory to ultimate world redemption. Six years of work and one year of rest are intended to invoke the messianic era that will begin at the end of the sixth millennium when the world as we know it, and the work we do in it, will also come to a halt; then the thousand years of Sabbath, or the messianic millennium, will begin.

And these unique years, as well as ultimate salvation, are indelibly bound up with the Land of Israel, both in terms of the fact that they are laws which apply exclusively to the holy land and that all our prophets insist that the acceptance of ethical monotheism and peaceful harmony by all nations of the world will be the result of Torah emanating from Jerusalem against the backdrop of a secure Israel.

All of these interpretations are fascinating, but I would like to suggest another more prosaic view. The biblical phrase, "a Sabbath unto God" for the Sabbatical year summarizes exactly how our land is different from all other lands: Jews in all lands are commanded to keep the Sabbath, but there is only one place in the world where even the land must keep the Sabbath (six years of work and one of rest) – here in Israel! The significance of the land keeping the Sabbath means that in the very essence of Israel's soil lies an expression of the divine will. In Israel, even the land is literally commanded to obey God's laws! God thereby becomes intimately involved in the very soil of the Land of Israel, something which does not happen anywhere else.

I would also add that every other country in the world

distinguishes the religious from the civic, the ritual from the cultural. Only in Israel dos there exist an opportunity for the Jew to express his culture and the culture of his environment in religious and Godly terms. Only in Israel can the Jew lead a life not of synthesis but of monothesis, not as a Jew at home and a cultural, national gentleman in the marketplace, but as a whole and seamless child of God and descendant of Abraham and Sarah. Here we have a unique opportunity to express our spiritual ideals in Mahane Yehuda as well as in the synagogue, in the theater as well as in the study hall.

A most profound vision of a Sabbatical and jubilee year: when Torah dominates not only the Synagogue and House of Study, but also the street and the banks, then all forms of slavery can be obliterated, debts can be rescinded, and everyone can be returned to his familial homestead. Only in Israel have we the potential to make God rule not only the ritual aspect of our lives, but the social, political and economic aspects as well. Only in Israel do we really have the potential of taking our every step – at home as well as in the street, in the synagogue as well as in the market place – in the presence of the divine.

Does Our Bible Condone Slavery?

> *If your brother becomes destitute and is then sold
> to you, you shall not make him work like a slave.*
>
> LEVITICUS 25:39

Indeed Judaism gave the world the idea and the ideal of freedom –
"I am the Lord thy God who took thee out of the land of Egypt, the house
of bondage" – how can we justify that our Bible accepts the institution
of slavery and even legislates proper and improper treatment of slaves?
Why didn't our Torah abolish slavery absolutely? If we compare the laws
of the Hebrew slave as found in *Mishpatim* (Ex. 21:2–6) to the laws of
the Hebrew slave as found in the portion of *Behar* (Lev. 25:39–47), our
analysis may lead to a meaningful answer to our questions.

At first blush, the two primary sources appear to be in conflict
with each other. The portion of *Mishpatim* tells us the following: First
of all, if one purchases a Hebrew slave, he may only be enslaved for six
years; he must be completely freed at the advent of the seventh year
(Ex. 21:2). Second, this passage permits the owner to provide the slave
with a gentile servant as his wife during his period of enslavement,

stipulating that the children of this union will remain the gentile slaves of the owner after the Hebrew slave (father) is freed (Ex. 21:4). Third, if the Hebrew slave desires to remain in bondage longer than the six-year period – "because he loves his master, his wife, his children" – he may continue to be enslaved "forever" according to the literal meaning of the text or until the jubilee fiftieth year, according to our Talmudic sages; however, he must first submit to having his ear pierced at the doorpost of the mezuzah, so that the message of God's dominion ("Hear O Israel the Lord is our God, the Lord is one"), rather than human mastery, is not lost upon him (Ex. 21:5, 6).

A very different picture seems to emerge from the passage in *Behar*. Here the Bible emphasizes the fact that we are not dealing with slavery as understood in ancient times, that when a person was struck by poverty, his dire circumstances would force him to sell himself into servitude. Rather, the Torah insists that a person may never be reduced to servitude, but must rather:

> Be like a hired residential worker with you, and he shall work with you until the jubilee fiftieth year…Because they are [also, no less than you] My servants whom I have taken out of the land of Egypt: they may not be sold as one sells a slave. You shall not rule over them harshly; you must fear your God.
>
> Leviticus 25:40, 2–43

You are not to have slaves, our text is proclaiming; you are merely to have hired residential workers!

After examining our text in *Behar* we find a number of interesting differences between this passage and the text in Exodus. First, there does not seem to be a time limit of six years; the length of time of employment would seem to depend upon the contract between employer and employee. Second, this passage does not seem to mention anything about the employer providing a gentile servant as wife. And third, our text does not ordain piercing of the ear for a longer stay of employment. It does tell us in no uncertain terms that our Bible does not compromise with slavery! It only provides for hired residential workers.

The Talmud (*Kiddushin* 14a) teaches that each of these biblical passages is dealing with a different kind of "servant": the first (in *Mishpatim*) is a criminal who must be rehabilitated, a thief who does not have the means to restore his theft to its proper owner. Such an individual is put "on sale" by the religious court, whose goal is to guide a family toward undertaking the responsibility of rehabilitation. After all, the criminal is not a degenerate, his crime is not a "high risk" or sexual offense, and it is hoped that a proper family environment which provides nurture as well as gainful employment (with severance pay at the end of the six-year period) will put him back on his feet. He is not completely free since the religious court has ruled that he must be "sold," but one can forcefully argue that such a "familial environment, half-way house" form of rehabilitation is far preferable to jail incarceration. The family must receive compensation – and this in the form of the work performed by the servant as well as the children who will remain after he is freed – and the criminal himself must be taught how to live respectfully in a free society.

The second passage in *Behar* deals with a very different situation, wherein an individual cannot find gainful employment and he is freely willing to sell the work of his hands. The Bible here emphasizes that there is absolutely no room for slavery in such a case; the person may only be seen as a hired, residential laborer, who himself may choose the duration of his contract and his "person" is not "owned" in any way by his employer. He cannot be "given" a wife, and of course any children he may father are exclusively his children and not his employer's children!

There may also be a second way of viewing these two passages. Rabbi Nahum Rabinowitz, Dean of Yeshivat Birkat Moshe, suggests that slavery, as well as polygamy, underwent serious revision within Jewish Law. There were many concepts which our Torah felt could only be introduced in stages, ideas which even the Israelite world was not ready to accept at the time of the Sinai revelation. The first passage in *Mishpatim* comes at the very dawn of Jewish history, still utilizing the term *eved* (slave or servant), but transforming its significance profoundly; it places a time limit for the service of rehabilitating a "criminal" and impresses upon him the value of freedom by piercing the ear of one who wishes to remain beyond the legislated time! The second passage is taught after Israel has begun to come of age, has learned the laws of the Sabbatical year and jubilee freedom, and is therefore ready to hear that slavery is abolished and a hired residential worker – whom we dare not treat in a servile manner – has taken its place.

Similarly, this development is true when it comes to a gentile slave. In the verses immediately following our passage under analysis, the Bible provides for such a status. After all, one is farsighted if he is one step beyond his generation, but becomes a "crackpot" once he takes that second step. Moreover, a gentile's slave status is actually the first stage in conversion to Judaism, since a gentile slave must be circumcised (if male), go to a *mikveh* for ritual immersion, and accept all the commandments except those positive commandments determined by time – and once he is freed he is fully Jewish.

The most ringing declaration of the approach of Halakha toward universal recognition of human freedom and equality is found in this passage from Maimonides:

> It is [biblically] permitted to treat a gentile slave in a servile manner. Despite the fact that this is the law, traits of piety and ways of wisdom ordain that a person be compassionate and pursue righteousness…. The [employer] must feed [the gentile slave] with all the food and drink [that he feeds himself]. He may not treat him with scorn or speak to him with excessive shouting or anger. He must speak to him calmly and always listen to his complaint. "Is it not true that the One who made me, made him and prepared us all from one womb?"
>
> Laws of Slaves 9:8

Beḥukkotai

A Vision of Transformation

> *And I will grant peace in the land, and you shall*
> *lie down, and none shall make you afraid. And*
> *I will cause evil beasts to cease from the land;*
> *neither shall the sword go through your land.*
>
> LEVITICUS 26:6

What kind of world will exist "at the end of the days," the period of the Messiah and human redemption? Will the basic structure of the universe, the rhythm of our lives remain exactly the same – the sixty minutes to the hour, two parts hydrogen to one part oxygen – with the only major difference being the miracle of a vast multitude of different drummers recognizing the One God and His chosen orchestral leader (Israel)?

If so, this means that our present realities can be sanctified, ennobled – but need not be utterly destroyed. Or will the messianic age have to inaugurate an entirely new world, an indelible change in the nature of the universe, radically different physics and physical existence? I would like to suggest that such not-only-theoretical speculation can be discerned as the preoccupation of the great sages of the Mishna, and their two alternate theological views give rise to two different translations of a word in this Torah reading.

The opening of *Behukkotai* sounds remarkably redolent of the messianic dream, the goal of human history. God promises the Israelites that if they but maintain His laws and commandments, their physical needs will be taken care of with good crops and good harvests, and the ever-present danger of wild animals will be removed:

> "And I will grant peace in the land, and you shall lie down, and none shall make you afraid. I will cause evil beasts to cease (*v'hishbati*) from the land; neither shall the sword go through your land."
>
> Leviticus 26:6

How are we to understand the concept: "cause to cease"? The Midrash (*Torat Kohanim*) records that Rabbi Yehuda defines *v'hishbati* as God causing these "evil beasts" to disappear from the world, that God will destroy them.

However, Rabbi Shimon interprets the word to mean that God will cause the evil of these beasts to cease: their evil nature will be destroyed, but the beasts themselves will not be destroyed.

Since this is not the only dispute recorded between these two sages, various commentaries have attempted to discern a more fundamental difference in their positions. For example, regarding the festival of Passover, our Bible commands:

> Seven days [of Passover] shall you eat unleavened bread; but by the first day you shall have caused the leaven to cease to exist (*tashbitu*) from your homes.
>
> Exodus 12:15

Clearly, the term for the "destruction" of leavening (*hametz*) is the same as the term for the "destruction" of wild beasts. And, true to form, we find the following difference of opinion in the Mishna:

Rabbi Yehuda rules there is no destruction except with fire, but the sages rule [including Rabbi Shimon] that [the leavened substance] may be turned into crumbs and scattered to the wind or thrown into the sea.

Pesaḥim 21a

According to the Rogachover Rebbe, their debate is primarily semantic: in terms of how to define the verb *sh-v-t*, which may best be translated "to cease to exist." Rabbi Shimon (as well as the majority of the sages) defines "*tashbitu*" as the destruction of the primary function: as long as the leavening is no longer edible or the wild beasts are no longer vicious, they can be considered to have been destroyed. Rabbi Yehuda, on the other hand, insists that destruction, or ceasing to exist, must include the substantive demolition of the object itself.

The Lubavitcher Rebbe, Rabbi Menahem Mendel Schneerson of blessed memory, reveals another ideological difference of opinion between these two sages. He suggests that they consistently differ as to what is more significant, the external action or the internal intention. For example, if an individual desecrates the Sabbath without having intended to do so – imagine he was washing his hands without realizing that the faucet he had turned on was directly above his business competitor's garden and he in fact was unintentionally causing the flowers to grow when he turned on the faucet – Rabbi Yehuda declares him culpable and Rabbi Shimon frees him from guilt. For the former it is the action that counts: a Jew ended up watering a garden on the Sabbath; for the latter it is the intention, and in our case in point he only intended to wash his hands.

They similarly disagree about garbage removal from the house to the public domain on the Sabbath: Rabbi Shimon frees the individual from biblical culpability, since he did not intend to use the garbage – the object of his act of carrying from domain to domain – and he therefore was not engaged in a meaningful creative activity; his only intent was to remove the garbage from his home, and not to derive benefit from it in any way. Rabbi Yehuda declares him guilty nevertheless, because after all he committed the act of carrying, and Halakha is not concerned about the reason for which he carried.

The final example relates to the problem of oil left over in a lamp which had been lit before the start of a festival. Rabbi Yehuda forbids use of this oil because when it had initially been lit, the householder put it out of his mind for festival use, thereby rendering it *muktzah*, forbidden to be moved until the end of the festival day. Rabbi Shimon, however, permits it, because now that the light has gone out, the householder can use the oil in a manner permitted on the festival, and permissibility for him is only dependent on present intent. In this light, the initial differences of opinion between them assume a different perspective. For Rabbi Shimon, as long as I no longer intend to eat the leavening or as long as the animals have no intent to damage, these objects in effect ceased to exist; for Rabbi Yehuda the act of destruction is the only way for the objects to cease to exist.

Building on the Lubavitcher Rebbe, I would like to place a slightly different spin on the disputes we have just catalogued from a more theological point of view. How does Judaism deal with the problem of evil in the world? Is evil an objective force which must be destroyed, or can even evil be uplifted and redeemed, if only we perceive the positive essence of every aspect of creation and utilize it for good? Rabbi Shimon truly believes that the ultimate task of the individual is to sanctify everything; he in effect cancels the concept of *muktzah* (set aside, not for Sabbath or festival use) from the religio-legal lexicon, maintaining that virtually everything can be brought within the domain of the sacred if the human mind only wishes to use it for such a purpose. Rabbi Shimon is after all the great mystic of Jewish tradition, the teacher of the *Zohar*, the advocate of uniting all worlds and uplifting even the most far-flung sparks; "there is no object devoid of holiness," teaches Jewish mysticism.

On the other hand, Rabbi Yehuda is not so optimistic and does recognize the existence of evil. Hence he emphasizes the biblical command "and you shall burn out the evil from their midst" (Deut. 17:7).

The period between Passover and Shavuot is the progressive count of days between the physical and incomplete redemption of the broken matza and our advancement after 49 days to the spiritual, all-embracing redemption of the Torah we received at Sinai. The *ḥametz* (leavening) is the symbol of that which swells and expands, of raw emotions and physical instincts; it is made to "cease to exist" by destruction on Passover.

On Shavuot, however, it will be sanctified, transformed into two holy loaves of *halla* (*hametz*) brought on the altar to God. What was forbidden (evil) seven weeks ago has now been redeemed. If anything, Shavuot is a manifestation of the redemption of evil, of our vision of the possibility of dedicating every aspect of our existence to God.

Rabbi Yehuda insisted on destroying the *hametz* on Passover, obliterating it from the world; Rabbi Shimon understood that it would only be necessary to re-route its function, to look at it in a different way.

Rabbi Yehuda insists that the evil beasts will be destroyed in the messianic period, a time when all that is evil will be obliterated from the earth; Rabbi Shimon maintains that the fundamental nature of the world will not change, the wild animals will still roam the forests, but their evil will be transformed, their force and vigor will be utilized positively. Rabbi Yehuda sees the millennium as devoid of Amalek, the nation bent on the destruction of Israel; our Bible commands us to "*destroy* the memory of Amalek" (Deut. 25:19). Perhaps Rabbi Shimon would indeed see the millennium as being devoid of the *memory* of the ancient Amalek, for Amalek at that time will repent and join forces with Israel. Does our Talmud (*Gittin* 57b) not record that the grandchildren of Haman (the Aggagi Amalekite) taught Torah in Bnei Brak?! I pray for the vision of Rabbi Shimon.

On What Merit Will We Be Redeemed?

> *And yet for all that, when they are in the land of*
> *their enemies, I will not reject them, neither will I*
> *abhor them, to destroy them utterly, and break My*
> *covenant with them; for I am the Lord their God.*
>
> LEVITICUS 26:44

*B*ehukkotai opens with issues of reward and punishment. The
Torah is fiercely insistent on the Israelites conducting their lives according to a very specific system of law. If they reject the path of the Torah,
the text unfolds a long litany of horrible consequences:

> I will appoint terror over you, even consumption and fever, that
> shall make the eyes fail, and the soul languish, and you shall sow
> your seed in vain, for your enemies shall eat it.
>
> Leviticus 26:16

However, although the general leitmotif of the Bible vis-à-vis the Israelites may aptly be summarized as "I never promised you a rose garden,"

there is one guarantee that the Almighty does give to the people of His covenant: Israel will never be completely destroyed, and eventually "the children shall return to their borders [of the Promised Land]" (Jer. 31:16). And so our difficult catalogue of chastisements concludes:

> But they will make amends for their sin. Then I will remember My covenant with Jacob, and also My covenant with Isaac, and also my covenant with Abraham will I remember, and I will remember the land.
>
> Leviticus 26:42

But why the reverse chronological order of Jacob, Isaac and Abraham? Would not the more logical, chronological order of Abraham, Isaac and Jacob been a more apt rendering of the text? Rabbi Zalman Sorotzkin, in his biblical commentary *Oznayim LaTorah*, discusses precisely this issue, and suggests that the various covenants alluded to in our biblical citation reflect varying degrees of merit required for our redemption, whereby the Bible moves from maximal to minimal merit as being necessary. In effect, God is comforting the Israelites, telling them that He will redeem them even if they are less than completely worthy!

Each of the Patriarchs is generally identified with a specific aspect of divine Service. Abraham represents lovingkindness and generosity (*hesed*) expressed in his tent which was opened on all four sides to accommodate any and every wanderer in the desert; Isaac represents personal sacrifice, even to the extent of his willingness to give up his life for his heritage (*akeda*); and Jacob represents dedication to the Torah as in the descriptive phrase "Jacob was a...dweller of tents" (Gen. 25:27), which the Midrash takes as the tent of Torah study, a reference to the fourteen years this youngest and most favored patriarch spent studying Torah in the yeshiva-tents of Shem and Ever.

Rabbi Sorotzkin ingeniously explains the reverse order in terms of God's decreasing expectations of the quality of merit necessary for our redemption. Optimally we should be redeemed on the basis of our total commitment to Torah, the vocation of Jacob-Israel, whose status as the most exemplary of the forefathers is eternalized in our nation's having been named Israel.

Falling short of that maximum and all-encompassing degree of commitment, the covenant of Isaac, the devotion of one who is ready to suffer for his faith, who experiences persecution and is ready to even give up his life if necessary, will also function as a viable means to bring the redemption. "It is sufficient that the mourner continues to mourn" in order for the Messiah to arrive, suggests the Talmud (*Sanhedrin* 97a). And indeed, Jews were transported to Auschwitz irrespective of whether or not they observed the laws of kashrut, irrespective of whether or not they were conversant with the Torah text.

And even if the only connection the Jewish people have with God is the loving hospitality of Abraham – as long as there exists within Israel an openness of spirit and generosity of the soul toward the poor, the widow, the orphan, and the stranger – for this alone will God remember His covenant with His eternal nation and restore us to our homeland.

Rabbi Sorotzkin then quotes from a letter he received from Rabbi Shmuel Dovid Walkin, who pointed out that the last phrase in the verse, "I will remember the land," constitutes a fourth category of commitment for the possibility of redemption. Even if the Jewish people have little dedication to Torah, are not suffering from persecution and do not major in acts of loving-kindness, but as long as they love the land of Israel, it will be considered sufficient by God to allow for the redemption. Rabbi Walkin found support for this idea from a verse in Psalms: "You will arise and have mercy on Zion, for it is time to favor her, for the appointed time has come" (Ps. 102:14). And what will bring the appointed time, the period of the Messiah? The answer appears in the very next verse: "Because Your servants take pleasure in her [Israel's] stones, and graciously love her [Israel's] dust" (102:15).

Rabbi Isaac HaLevi Herzog, former Ashkenazi Chief Rabbi of Israel, was once commenting on the Talmudic passage concerning redemption that speaks of the Messiah arriving on a donkey (*Sanhedrin* 98a). Why a donkey and not a horse? Why a donkey and not "on the wings of eagles" or on the wings of an airplane? Why a donkey and not a Volvo? Rabbi Herzog explained that most creatures go a certain distance, stop to rest for a while, and then continue moving. The donkey, however, often stops after a while and refuses to continue to progress, no matter how much prodding (or kicking) he may receive; sometimes he even goes backward for some inexplicable reason. Ultimately, however, the donkey reaches its destination.

The Torah would like us to develop from covenant to covenant, to perhaps begin with commitment to land but then to progress to commitment to lovingkindness, to the willingness to suffer persecution and eventually to total involvement in Torah. However, even if we begin only with the most minimal commitment to land, and stop without going further just like the donkey, this too should prove sufficient to restore us to our homeland. This explains the merit of the early twentieth-century Zionists, many of whom may not have been observant, but nevertheless it was their love of the land which paved the way for our period of the beginning of the flowering of our redemption.

*   *   *

A Postscript as to What is Necessary for Redemption

A second verse in the portion of *Beḥukkotai*, particularly when it is compared to the text in the Grace After Meals, further illuminates the kinds of steps that must be taken for the redemptive process to become part of our lives: "And I am the Lord your God; I have taken you from the land of Egypt where you were slaves ... And I have broken the pegs of your yoke, and led you upright" (Lev. 26:13).

When we turn to the Grace After Meals, we find, after the fourth blessing and within a section of petitions to God each of which begins with "The Compassionate One (*HaRaḥaman*)", a request apparently based on the verse just cited: "The Compassionate One! May He break the yoke of oppression from our necks and lead us upright in our land."

Why is it that in the biblical verse we read of God's breaking the pegs of our yoke (of oppression), whereas in the parallel petition in the Grace After Meals we read: "The Compassionate One! May He break the yoke of oppression" mentioning the yoke and leaving out the pegs!

Rashi explains that these pegs (*motot* in Hebrew) "are a kind of peg inserted in both ends of the yoke which hold back the strap from slipping off the head of the ox whereby the knot might become undone."

The late and revered Torah teacher in London, Rabbi Isaac Bernstein, quoted Rabbi Shlomo Zalman Ullman, one of the leading rabbis of Romania before World War 11, who explained that at the end of each planting season, the owner of the oxen saves the 'yoke' for the next season – but usually not the pegs. However, if he is going to quit farming altogether and move to the city, then at the end of the season he not only gets rid of the pegs, but he rids himself of the yoke as well. He simply has no use for it next season, because as far as he is concerned there is to be no next season.

Rabbi Ullman taught that the verse in *Beḥukkotai* refers to the period after the First Temple, the First Exile. Therefore the Torah speaks in terms of breaking the pegs because of the fact that there would still be a "next season," a second exile, and the yoke of exile would still be upon us. However, our prayer in the Grace After Meals is concerned with the period after the Second Temple, and our petition is that God should bring us back to the land, walking upright, and that our yoke of oppression should be thrown away altogether and forever, completely and irrevocably. After all, there are only two destructions mentioned in the Torah – not a third! (One in Leviticus, *Beḥukkotai* and one in Deuteronomy, *Ki Tavo*.)

Finally, we find two textual traditions for the concluding part of the petition from the Grace After Meals that we've just been discussing: one is the familiar, "And may He lead us upright *to* our land (*l'artzeinu*)," and the second version reads "And may He lead us upright *in* our land (*b'artzeinu*)."

How are we to understand the difference between these two versions, each highlighting a different preposition?

I'd like to suggest that for those who live outside the land of Israel, the appropriate version to be recited is that we be brought "upright to our land." Our prayer to God is then the most basic of all: We want to enter Israel standing straight, on our two feet, vertically, as opposed to horizontally, as are those brought to be buried in Israel inside a coffin. Arriving in the land standing tall and erect means that we want to come while alive, when we can still work, accomplish, contribute.

The prayer must be slightly but profoundly emended for those who live in Israel. We have said earlier, very often the first impulse that drove the founders of the State of Israel during the first and second *aliyot* was their powerful love of the land. Without it, they would have never arrived. And with it, they were able to refashion the malaria infested swamps of the Galilee and the burning deserts of the Negev into cities and villages, parks and gardens, recreational malls and business centers.

But alas, love of the land is only the beginning; a first, albeit significant, step. Love of the land may be enough for redeeming the soil from its natural enemies of swamps and mosquitos and discovering ways of providing it with water and minerals; but love of the land alone is not enough for the redemption of the nation and the world. For us to reach that stage, it is necessary for the Israelite inhabitants of the land to become a light unto the nations of the world – first, by establishing a government based on justice and compassion for all, then by expressing our willingness to sacrifice for our country and our ideals, and finally, by establishing a democratically desired Torah-true society. In order to accomplish this, the citizenry of Israel must believe in themselves and in their right to be in the Middle East, and must have a strong commitment to their Jewish identity and traditions: We must walk upright and proud *within* our land. This is the text we must use in Israel, and this is the way to bring the Messiah.

Biblical Commentators Cited in this Volume

Mishnaic Era

Onkelos HaGer. Disciple of Rabbi Eliezer and Rabbi Yehoshua, two of the great rabbis from the Tannaitic period. His famous translation of the Torah into Aramaic is known simply as *The Targum*.

Yonatan ben Uziel. Disciple of the famed Tanna, Hillel. Noted biblical translator, whose Western Aramaic translations include many Midrashic tales.

11th Century

Yitzhaki, Shlomo. RASHI (France, 1040–1105). Our foremost commentator on the Torah and the Talmud.

12th Century

Halevi, Yehuda (Spain, 1075–1141). Noted Torah scholar and poet. Author of the *Kuzari*.

Ibn Ezra, Abraham (Spain, 1089–1164). Noted poet and grammarian. Author of commentary to the Bible.

Maimonides, Moshe ben Maimon. RAMBAM (Spain & Egypt, 1135–1204). Author of *Mishneh Torah*, a comprehensive halakhic code of Jewish law; and of the famous philosophical treatise *Guide for the Perplexed*.

Shmuel ben Meir. RASHBAM (France, 1080–1158). Grandson of Rashi, one of the Ba'alei Tosafot. Author of commentary to the Torah.

13ᵗʰ Century

Meiri, Menachem ben Solomon (Provence, 1249–1316). Talmudic scholar and commentator. Summarized the teachings of his predecessors of the previous three centuries in *Beit Habehira*, a digest of commentary on the Talmud and the Halakha derived from it.

Nahmanides, Moshe ben Nahman. RAMBAN (Spain, 1194–1270). Famous biblical commentator and Talmudist. His biblical commentary will often quote the commentaries of Rashi and Ibn Ezra.

15ᵗʰ Century

Abarbanel, Don Isaac (Spain & Italy, 1437–1508). Noted statesman and minister for kings of Spain, Portugal and Italy. Author of commentaries to the Bible, the Passover Haggada and Pirkei Avot.

Arama, Yitzhak (Spain, 1420–1494). Author of *Akedat Yitzhak*.

16–17ᵗʰ Century

Eidels, Shmuel Eliezer Halevy. MAHARSHA (Krakow, 1555–1631). Renowned rabbi and Talmudist famous for his commentaries on the Talmud, *Hiddushei Halakhot* and *Hiddushei Aggadot*.

Heller, Yom Tov Lipman (Bavaria & Krakow, 1578–1654). Rabbi and talmudist, best-known for writing a commentary on the Mishna called the *Tosafot Yom Tov* (1614–7). One of the major Talmudic scholars in Prague and in Poland during the "Golden Age" before 1648.

Horowitz, Isaiah. **Shelah HaKadosh** (Prague & Israel, 1565–1630). Noted Kabbalist. Author of *Shnei Luḥot Habrit*.

Isserles, Moshe. REMA (Krakow, 1520–1572). Author of *Mapa* (Tablecloth), representing the Ashkenazi Torah world, and integrated it with the *Shulḥan Arukh*, enabling it to represent the entire Jewish Torah spectrum; and of *Darkhei Moshe*, a commentary on the "Tur."

Karo, Joseph (Toledo & Safed, 1488–1575). Author of *Beit Yosef*, an extensive survey of relevant halakhic literature, from the Talmud down to works of his contemporaries. His halakhic decisions were codified in his *Shulḥan Arukh*.

Lunchitz, Shlomo Efraim (Poland & Bohemia, 1550–1619). Author of the popular commentary on the Torah, *Kli Yakar*.

Seforno, Ovadiah (Italy, 1470–1550). Author of commentary to the Bible.

Vital, Haim (Safed & Damascus, 1543–1620). A student of kabbala, disciple of the holy Ari, Rabbi Isaac Luria.

18th Century

Berditchev, Levi Yitzhak ben Meir (Poland, 1740–1810). Founder of Hassidism in Central Poland. Author of *Kedushat Levi* commentary to the Bible.

Falk, Yaakov Yehoshua (Poland & Germany, 1680–1756). One of the greatest Talmudists of his time; his book of commentary and novellae on the Talmud, *P'nei Yehoshua*, is a classic work of the era of *aḥaronim*.

Pardo, David (Italy, 1719–1792). Author of *Maskil LeDavid*, a commentary on Rashi.

Shneur Zalman of Liadi. Ba'al HaTanya (Russia, 1745–1812). Famed scholar in both Talmud and Kabbalah. Founder of Habad Hassidism. Author of the halakhic work known as *Shulḥan Arukh HaRav*, and of *Likutei Amarim*, referred to as the *Tanya*.

Yaakov Yosef of Polonnoye (Poland, 1710–1784). Student of the Baal

Shem Tov and author of *Toledot Yaakov Yosef*, a masterful defense of Hassidut and a scathing indictment of rabbinic (mitnagdic) leadership.

19th Century

Berlin, Naftali Tzvi Yehuda. NETZIV (Russia, 1817–1893). Head of the famous Yeshiva of Volozhin. Author of commentary to the Torah called *Ha'amek Davar*.

Bornsztain, Avrohom. AVNEI NEZER (Poland, 1839–1910). Rabbi of Sochatchov. Author of *Avnei Nezer*, a posthumously-published set of Torah responsa.

Epstein, Yechiel Michel (1829–1908). Author of *Arukh HaShulḥan*, a halakhic work which traces the origins of each law and custom to its source.

HaKohen, Meir Simha (Russia, 1843–1926). Rabbi of Dvinsk. Outstanding author and Talmudic scholar. Author of biblical commentary *Meshekh Ḥokhma*, and also of a commentary to the Rambam's *Mishneh Torah* called *Ohr Sameaḥ*.

Hirsch, Samson Rafael (Germany, 1808–1888). Author of six-volume commentary to the Torah, originally written in German.

Kagan, Yisrael Meir (Poland, 1839–1933). Famous rabbinical scholar who lived in the town of Radin, and refused to accept any official positon in the rabbinate. His most famous works are the *Ḥafetz Ḥaim*, which details all the laws against slandering one's fellow Jew; and his six-volume halakhic treatise called *Mishna Berura*.

Kotzk, Menahem Mendel (Poland, 1787–1859). Noted scholar and disciple of Rav Simha Bunim of Pshiskha.

Mecklenburg, Ya'akov (Germany, 1785–1865). Served as Chief Rabbi of Koenigsberg. Author of famous biblical commentary *HaKtav VehaKabbala*.

Rabinowitz, Tzadok Hakohen (Lublin, 1823–1900). One of the most prolific authors in the history of the Hassidic movement. Having excelled in both the Hassidic and non-Hassidic world, Rav Tzadok's writings became a synthesis of analytical logic and mysticism. Eventually, some of his classes were transcribed and compiled into a work known as *Pri Tzaddik*.

Salanter, Israel Lipkin (Eastern Europe, 1809–1883). Founder of the Mussar movement.

Schneerson, Menahem Mendel (Russia, 1789–1866). One of the great Torah scholars of his generation. Grandson of the Ba'al HaTanya, and third leader of the Lubavitch Hassidic movement. His series of halakhic responsa is called *Tzemaḥ Tzedek*.

20th Century

Abramsky, Yehezkel (Grodno, London & Jerusalem, 1886–1976). Eminent Orthodox rabbi, who headed the London Beth Din for 17 years, and author of *Ḥazon Yeḥezkel*, a twenty-four volume commentary on the *Tosefta*.

Bernstein, Isaac (London, 1931–1994). Outstanding orator and Torah scholar. Famous for his weekly Torah lessons, which were later assembled and distributed as a series of tapes.

Elon, Menachem (Israel, 1923–). A prolific author on halakha, he served as a judge on the Israeli Supreme Court and as its deputy president (1988–1993), and his opinions often draw upon the principles of Jewish law.

Herzog, Isaac Halevy (Ireland & Israel, 1889–1959). Rabbinical authority and author of numerous books and articles on halakhic problems relating to the Torah and the State of Israel. Served as rabbi of Belfast, and then Dublin, Ireland from 1916 to 1922. Went on to serve as Chief Rabbi of Ireland from 1922 to 1936, when he immigrated to Palestine to become Ashkenazi Chief Rabbi following the death of Rabbi Abraham Isaac HaKohen Kook.

Hutner, Yitzchok (Warsaw & Jerusalem, 1906–1980). Founder and Rosh Yeshiva of Pachad Yitzchok in Har Nof, Jerusalem, Mesivta Rabbi Chaim Berlin and Kollel Gur Aryeh. Recognizing the critical importance of creating well-rounded disciples prepared to communicate the power and depth of Judaism he concentrated his efforts in this area. His discourses on Shabbat and festivals, *Paḥad Yitzḥak*, were compiled in seven volumes.

Kaminetzky, Yaakov (Toronto & New York, 1891–1986). Head of Torah VaDa'as Yeshiva. Author of *Emet LeYaakov*.

Karelitz, Avrohom Yeshayahu. CHAZON ISH (Belarus & Bnei Brak, 1878–1953). A scholar devoted to the study of the Torah and Talmud, although also a student of the sciences, since knowledge of these subjects is necessary for a full understanding of various aspects of Jewish law and practice. Author of *Ḥazon Ish* (his magnum opus). Not appointed as communal leader, yet enormously influential on the life and institutions of religious Jewry, especially in Palestine where he immigrated in 1933. He did not publish many responsa, but became a supreme authority on halakha.

Kook, Abraham Isaac HaKohen (Jaffa & Jerusalem, 1865–1935). Founder of the Israel Chief Rabbinate. Author of many philosophical works and a commentary to the prayer book called *Olat Re'aya*.

Leibowitz, Yeshayahu (Jerusalem, 1903–1994). Israeli philosopher and scientist known for his outspoken, often controversial opinions on Judaism, ethics, religion and politics. Editor of *Encyclopaedia Hebraica* in its early stages.

Rosen, Yosef (Rogachov, Belarus & Vienna, 1858–1936), the Rogachover Rebbe. Also known by the name of his main work *Tzafenat Pa'n eaḥ*; prominent Talmudic scholar of the early 20th century.

Schneerson, Menahem Mendel (New York, 1902–1994). Seventh rebbe of Habad Hassidim. Noted Torah scholar and author of *Likutei Siḥos*," insights into the weekly portion with emphasis on Rashi's commentary.

Soloveitchik, Aaron (Chicago, 1917–2001). Noted Talmudic scholar and halakhic authority. Head of Yeshivas Brisk in Chicago. Younger brother of Rabbi Joseph B. Soloveitchik.

Soloveitchik, Joseph B. (Boston, 1903–1993). Master Talmud teacher, Yeshiva University. Author of numerous philosophical and halakhic works including *Ish Hahalakha* (*Halakhic Man*) and *The Lonely Man of Faith*. Famed worldwide for his lectures in Talmud and biblical exegesis, and credited with being a major interpreter of Modern Orthodoxy.

Sorotzkin, Zalman (Lithuania & Israel, 1881–1966). Author of *Oznayim LaTorah*, a commentary on the Torah, and *Moznayim LaTorah*,"on the festivals.

Ullman, Shlomo Zalman (Romaniam 1865–1930). Authow of *Yerios Shlomo* and one of the leading rabbis of Romania before World War II.

Zevin, Shlomo Yosef (Minsk & Israel, 1888–1978). Eminent Orthodox rabbi and founder of the *Encyclopedia Talmudit*, a Hebrew halakhic encyclopedia.

Index of Biblical & Talmudic Sources

Gen 1	114	Ex 1:5	236
Gen 1:1	166	Ex 12	205
Gen 1:2	114–5	Ex 12:2	67
Gen 1:27	138, 210	Ex 12:15	256
Gen 2:16, 17	95	Ex 13:8	204
Gen 2:17	107	Ex 18:8	204
Gen 3:16	107	Ex 19:13	241
Gen 3:18–19	96	Ex 20:2	166
Gen 4:4	28	Ex 21:2-6	249
Gen 5:2	138	Ex 21:4	250
Gen 6:7	16	Ex 21:5, 6	250
Gen 6:9	211-212	Ex 21:10	225
Gen 8:21	28	Ex 21:19	145
Gen 9:5	144	Ex 22:6–14	177
Gen 12:3	236	Ex 23:19	94
Gen 15:7	81-2	Ex 23:25	43
Gen 15:7–8	82	Ex 24:9, 10	204
Gen 17:4, 5	236	Ex 24:7-10	210, 229
Gen 28:12	236	Ex 24:10	228
Gen 35:22	91	Ex 25:8	60
Gen 39:6	95	Ex 29:43	90
Gen 49:9	51	Ex 34:29	9
		Ex 34:33	11

Ex 34:6	63, 192	Lev 19:2	153
		Lev 19:17	160
Lev 1:1	5, 9	Lev 19:18	165
Lev 1:2	13, 19, 20, 21	Lev 20:2	75
Lev 1:3–4	23	Lev 21:1	175
Lev 1:9	27, 28, 29	Lev 21:10	181
Lev 4:2	38	Lev 22:28–33	187
Lev 4:3	38	Lev 22:32	185, 186, 189, 191
Lev 4:13–14	31, 34, 38	Lev 23:1–2	195
Lev 4:15, 16	38	Lev 23:15	199, 203
Lev 4:22	39	Lev 23:15–16	203, 209, 227
Lev 4:24	37	Lev 23:17	228
Lev 6:1–2	49	Lev 23:23	215
Lev 6:17–18	54	Lev 25:4–5	225
Lev 7:18	57, 58	Lev 25:1–5	223
Lev 8:35–36	61	Lev 25:8	227, 243
Lev 9:1	67	Lev 25:9–10,	24 240
Lev 10:1–2	71, 77	Lev 25:10	225, 235, 237, 239
Lev 10:2	59, 81, 85	Lev 25:13	226
Lev 10:3	70, 79, 89, 128	Lev 25:38	245
Lev 10:9	129	Lev 25:39	249
Lev 10:10	72	Lev 25:39–47	249
Lev 11:2–3	93, 94	Lev 25:40, 2–43	250
Lev 12:1, 2	106	Lev 26:6	233, 255, 256
Lev 12:2	101, 105	Lev 26:13	264
Lev 12:3	106, 109	Lev 26:16	261
Lev 12:2–4	105, 106	Lev 26:42	262
Lev 12:6–7	113	Lev 26:44	261
Lev 14:34	117, 118		
Lev 14:36, 37	118	Num 5:7	37
Lev 14:37	119	Num 14:23	129
Lev 16:1	127	Num 13:33	130
Lev 16:4	131		
Lev 16:30	133, 135	Deut 5:12, 14	210
Lev 17:14	94	Deut 5:131	169
Lev 18:5	137, 139, 143, 151, 188	Deut 6:18	155
Lev 18:21	75, 149	Deut 11:13	43
		Deut 17:7	258

Deut 18:10	75	Zefaniah 3:9	237
Deut. 21:15–17	91	Hosea 2:21	225
Deut 25:19	259		
Deut 26:1, 2	228	Micah 4	171
Deut 26:5-13	202, 228, 229		
Deut 26:9, 10	229	Ps 83:2, 3	83
		Ps 92:1	233-4
Joshua 1:8	177	Ps 102:14	263
		Ps 102:15	263
I Sam 1:13	39	Ps 115:12–13	194
		Ps 115:16	15
II Sam 6:7	59	Ps 119:126	79
II Sam 6:21	73	Ps 130:1	55
II Sam ch. 12	39	Ps 150:3	216
I Kings 18:37–40	102	Prov 27:10	167
I Kings 19:2	103	Prov 31:10–31	130
II Kings 4:11	122	Prov 31:15	130˙
II Kings 5:1	122	Prov 31:20	130
II Kings 5:13–14	121	Prov 31:21	130
II Kings 5:15	122		
II Kings 5:27	123	Song of Songs 4:1	167
II Kings 20:13	201	I Chron 22:8	73
Is 1:10–15	38	II Chron 32:25-29	201
Is 1:26	33		
Is 2	171	**Mishna**	
Is 40:3	6	Mishna Avot 3:17	90
Is 44:25	171	Mishna Kritut 1:1	34
		Mishna Rosh Hashana 4:1	216
Jer 2:2	6	Mishna Yoma 8:9	135
Jer 7:21–22	62		
Jer 7:23	62	**Babylonian Talmud**	
Jer 9:22, 23	64	Arakhin 16b	161–2
Jer 34:13–14	62	Bava Metzia 83b	160
		Bekhorot 29b	32
Ez 44:15–24	182	Berakhot 34a	44
Ez 44:24	176	Berakhot 35a	15

Berakhot 26a   58
Berakhot 26b   42
Berakhot 28b   159
Berakhot 34b   57
Gittin 57b   259
Gittin 90b   225
Horayot 3b   34
Horayot 6b   34
Ḥullin 89a   91
Ketubot 5   225
Ketubot 110b   245
Kiddushin 2a   224
Kiddushin 14a   251
Kiddushin 49b–50a   57
Kritut 5a   58
Menaḥot 110a   29
Nedarim 28a   57
Nidda 31b   110
Pesaḥim 8a   60
Pesaḥim 21a   257
Pesaḥim 109a   86
Rosh Hashana 26a   241
Rosh Hashana 29b   216
Rosh Hashana 33b   216
Sanhedrin 13b, 14a   32
Sanhedrin 64   75
Sanhedrin 70a–b   86
Sanhedrin 74a, b   189, 190
Sanhedrin 94a   200, 201
Sanhedrin 98a   263
Shabbat 31   167
Shabbat 31a   168
Shabbat 33b   231, 233

Shabbat 34a   233
Shabbat 132a   109
Yevamot 62b   169, 170
Yoma 23a   63
Yoma 66a   186
Yoma 69b   50
Yoma 85a, b   151
Yoma 85b   139

Jerusalem Talmud

Nedarim 9:4   165

Maimonides – Mishneh Torah

Laws of the Foundations
of Torah 5:1   188, 192, 193
Laws of the Foundations
of Torah 5:2   192
Laws of the Foundations
of Torah 5:10   192
Laws of the Foundations
of Torah 5:11   186
Laws of Ḥametz and Matza 7:1   204
Laws of Kings 4:10   183
Laws of Kings ch. 11, 12   32
Laws of Kings 5:1, 4   193
Laws of the Impurity of
Tzara'at 16:10   118
Laws of the Lulav 8:15   87
Laws of Murder 1:4   145
Laws of Prayer 1:1   42
Laws of Repentance 1:1   37
Laws of Slaves 9:8   252
Laws of Yesodei Hatorah 5:10   140

The fonts used in this book are from the Arno family